Lee's Trailer Park

Lee's Trailer Park

... overcoming adversity in life

by: J. H. James

Lee's Trailer Park—overcoming adversity in life
Copyright © 2022 by J. H. James.

All rights reserved. No part of this publication may be reproduced, distributed, or transmitted in any form or by any means, including photocopying, recording, or other electronic or mechanical methods, without the prior written permission of the publisher, except in the case of brief quotations embodied in critical reviews and certain other noncommercial uses permitted by copyright law.

ISBN: 978-1-7360474-1-5

Acknowledgment

My thanks to my best friend and blood-brother for reading through the initial drafts of this book and helping to keep me on track.

Dedication

To the woman who came into my life and made me the happiest man in the world . . . my wonderful wife, Ashlee. All of my love, forever, forever, forever . . . and a day.

Jesse "J.H." James
Website: www.jamesconsultingllc.com
Contact: jesse@jamesconsultingllc.com

FOREWORD

FULL DISCLOSURE

I have written this book under the quasi-pseudonym "J. H. James." My given name is Jesse H. James. While I like my birth name and have kept it throughout my life, I wanted to avoid any distraction by using the name Jesse James on the cover of the book and having it conjure up images of the wild west outlaw or the motorcycle guy who ended up in a messy divorce with Sandra Bullock. My goal was to maintain a positive approach at the outset and to limit my readers' minds from wandering before they even opened the cover.

That having been said, I now feel obligated to share the real story behind my name and how it was bestowed upon me since you've already made it to the first page! When I was born, my father's name was Jesse James II. My grandfather's name was Jesse James Jr., and I was in line to become Jesse James III. Naturally, the men in the family wanted me to pass that baton forward.

Well, my mom, being the resolute, perceptive, and determined person she was, would have no part of my carrying the moniker Jesse James throughout my time on this planet. She explained to my father and my grandfather that if I had that name, other children would pick on me while I was growing up. I'd endure bullying and end up in fights.

J. H. JAMES

My grandfather was a businessman and was used to negotiating win-win situations. He pulled my mom aside and said to her, "If you name him Jesse James, I will give you fifty dollars." (A significant sum of money back in those days!) Mom smiled and responded, "You know, it has a nice ring to it!" The rest is history, as they say.

Just for the record, my mom was a fighter and had a penchant for getting her way. Her idea of pulling a victory out of a loss was to call me "Jimmy," which she and our immediate family members did until the day she passed. Imagine: Thank goodness it didn't take hold outside of our home. "Jimmy James." I don't think so!

I survived the bullying and name-calling and had my lunchbox taken from me more times than I can remember. I also eventually learned how to protect myself and to hold onto my lunchbox. The thick skin I developed came in handy as I negotiated all the twists, turns, and challenges that life had to offer . . . both personally and professionally.

"Out of every adversity springs a seed of an equivalent or greater benefit." —Napoleon Hill

I hope you enjoy reading this book as much as I have enjoyed revisiting my early past and writing about it for you. More about my later years in a future book.

—J. H. James

CHAPTER ONE — THE JOURNEY BEGINS

BEFORE ME

It's where we are headed to, not where we've been, that determines who we become.

My mom was the youngest of five children. She had a sister and three brothers. They were raised together in a small two-story house in Queens, Long Island, before eventually going their separate ways.

My grandfather was a self-employed carpenter, and my grandmother raised the brood. They were hopelessly poor but somehow were able to survive while raising their children during the Depression. My grandfather once said to the kids, "If you hear a burglar during the night, get up and help him look for some money. Maybe if he finds something he will split it with us!"

Mom left home when she was sixteen due to a fight with my grandfather over a toothbrush. I have no clue what the real issue was or what other underlying circumstances could have caused that event to snap their relationship. What I do know is that my grandfather was a demanding disciplinarian and my mom was staunchly independent, which probably had a lot to do with their ultimate conflict.

She went to work in New York City as an elevator operator in an office building during the day and a cigarette girl in a nightclub in the evening. Between the two jobs, she made enough money to rent her own room and provide the necessities of life for herself.

It wasn't long after she was on her own in the world that she met my father-to-be in the nightclub where she hawked cigarettes. She married at the tender age of seventeen. The sailor and the cigarette girl—what a story! And I was the eventual byproduct of that marriage.

AFTER ME

My childhood wasn't what most would call idyllic, but it was memorable, and those memories are vivid in my mind's eye even today.

My father was in the Navy and my mom was a stay-at-home housewife. We lived in a government-owned Quonset hut development in Green Cove Springs, Florida. It was in the middle of a rural farm area where it wasn't uncommon for my dad to run out to the front porch in the middle of the night with a broom in his hand to ward off unwelcomed cows or hogs that were far too curious or aggressive for his liking.

Mom and Dad did not get along very well. She tried her best, but he was an adulterous cad who disrespected her and verbally abused her consistently, not to mention the emotional pain inflicted by her having to endure his blatant womanizing. They screamed at each other frequently. I'm certain that this is where I learned some very colorful language at a far-too early stage in my life. In fact, my parroting of language that I had been exposed to in our house resulted in my father washing out my mouth with a bar of soap one day—a punishment eternally etched into my memory, though I was only four years old at the time.

Another incident that I can clearly remember while living in the Quonset hut is the time when my father had slammed the car door of our green 1948 Plymouth on my mom's hand as she was getting into our car. I've always assumed it was unintentional at best and just plain mindless at worst. (They hadn't been arguing, and he was in a hurry to finish all of their errands before he went out that evening.) I can still hear her screams of pain in my mind, even now. Over the course of a week, the fingers on her left hand turned purple, and she lost two fingernails completely. To this very day, I watch intently as I close the car door for my wife when she enters or exits the car!

Then there was the day I fell off of my tricycle and landed on a nest of Florida fire ants, something that will also remain seared into my mind (and elsewhere) forever. Mom grabbed me in an instant and ran back to our Quonset hut in a flash—Olympic speed. She turned on the shower head in the tub and threw me into the healing stream of cold water to rid me of the unbearable pain caused by the biting ants.

I remember the noisy trucks that rolled through the Quonset hut development from time to time, dispersing pesticide spray to kill off the mosquito population and other unwanted insects. I wish they had gotten those fire ants before I fell off my tricycle! Sometimes I think of all that pesticide fog . . . It's no small wonder that I ended up with asthma! I can still see my father building a tent of sheets over my bed and turning on the vaporizer. The hissing and spitting sound of the brown, hot, steamy medicine was scary, but it was the price that had to be paid to feel the relief the powerful medicine provided. At least I could breathe!

One day, my mom took me to the grocery store with her. Inside the store was a bright-red Coca-Cola machine, an antique by today's standards. You put a nickel in the coin slot and pressed down on the silver steel lever, which released a small bottle of Coca-Cola in the bin below the lever. I loved Coca-Cola and decided that I wanted one immediately, at that place and time. My mom said, "No!" and I reacted by throwing a loud tantrum with all the obligatory crying and screaming necessary to get my point across. I wanted Coca-Cola, and I wanted it right then and there! Not giving into my tantrum, Mom put me in a one-armed body hold and yanked me from the grocery carriage in an instant—similar to the technique she employed when removing me from the nest of fire ants, absent the concern and compassion for my immediate well-being. This was the first day of my life that I fully realized Mom was the boss and that future tantrums or demands would be exercises in futility. I understood: No Coca-Cola for you!

During a Florida hurricane, we were all evacuated from the Quonset hut development and taken to the naval base hospital for safety purposes. For some strange reason (which I will never be able to figure out) my mom placed me on a top bunk bed instead of one of the bottom ones. Maybe I prompted her decision by asking to be put up there, thinking it would be cool to look down at everyone instead of the other way around. Whatever the cause, the result was not a positive one. During the evening, while sleeping, I rolled off the top bunk and landed on my head! The only good news is that we were already at the hospital, so the doctor's care, stitches, and wound dressings were administered quickly. This accident is probably the reason I have to write things down on a list today when I need to get more than two items at the store.

On Saturday evenings, we would go to the Jacksonville naval base to watch movies. All the sailors and their families sat out on the huge dock where their ships were moored. A white screen was erected, and the 8mm projector began humming away. On some Saturdays, I remember my father not being there with us to watch the movies. I guess he had more important things to deal with on those evenings ... somewhere else to be ... with someone other than us.

THE SPLIT

The predictable ending to my parents' matrimonial tragedy ultimately arrived. I can still clearly remember my mom packing our suitcases and throwing me under her arm again (which was becoming as strong as a lumberjack's) as we walked out on my Dad, leaving what little we had in the way of a family behind us forevermore. I was only four years old. Little did I know that I would never see my father, nor have any contact with him, for more than thirty years.

Because of the childhood trauma of their split-up, I seem to have developed the capacity to remember many incidents and events from long ago that others would have most likely left behind in the shadows of their past. I believe, however, that this ability to recall so many early childhood events and experiences is more a reflection of how my mind handled very stressful situations than a sign of my intellectual capacity to remember events.

Different people react to stress or trauma in different ways. Some people block certain memories or events as a matter of self-protection. For me, my detailed memories have been a means of keeping in touch with my past to prevent it from being lost forever.

THE FARMHOUSE AND BEYOND

I remember that my mom and I ended up staying in a small one-room apartment after we left my father. While my sense of the time frame is fuzzy, I know that it wasn't very long until she and I boarded a bus for a destination unknown to me!

Eventually, the bus stopped on the side of the road where the driver opened the door and let us out . . . and waited ever so briefly. I could see a dirt road and a farmhouse on the other side of the two-lane paved road.

J. H. JAMES

My mom helped me off the bus, handed me my suitcase, and then turned me over to the two people standing at the entrance to the dirt road. They owned the farm where I would now be living. Mom hugged me and said, "Don't worry, they will take good care of you. I will come back and get you soon." I was confused and overwhelmed with sadness and fear.

I remember walking down the dirt road with my two new care providers and looking over my shoulder with a heavy heart and tears in my eyes. I watched as the bus pulled away from the side of the road, headed into the distance with my mom somewhere inside of it.

My memory of the number of weeks I stayed at the farm is also vague. I do, however, remember thinking of my mom every day and praying for her to return every night before I went to sleep.

It was a morning ritual for me to go downstairs and look out the front door toward the dirt road that led from the highway to the farmhouse. Time and time again . . . no Mom in sight.

While I was at the farm, certain events helped to keep me preoccupied so that the absence of my mom would not consume me all day long. Every morning we (there were several other kids staying there besides me) would gather for breakfast and then join in on the daily chores.

We would first head to the henhouse and collect the eggs that had been laid overnight. Then it was on to milking the cows, feeding the pigs, and cleaning our room. There were a lot of single beds, all neatly arranged in an orderly fashion, in the same large room. (Thankfully, there were no upper bunks!)

One day, the farmer, accompanied by a few other men, brought me out to the pigpen. He pointed to a large hog, which was quickly pulled from its section of the pen. The men tied the hog to a fence post some distance away from the pen. It was then that I noticed the rifle!

Once the hog was totally secured to the post, everyone moved back to safety. The farmer raised his rifle and pointed it at the hog. BLAM! The hog slumped in position and became still.

The farmer quartered the hog, and we all helped carry the remnants of what was once a whole living animal into the farmhouse. His wife then trimmed out the different parts of the hog and placed some of them into the refrigerator with the rest heading to a freezer.

I wondered if I would ever eat bacon again! That turned out to be just a fleeting thought as I ate delicious fresh bacon, sausage, and eggs for breakfast the next morning!

Finally, the day arrived when I looked out the front door of the farmhouse and froze as I watched my mom walking down the dirt road leading from the highway to the farm. My instincts kicked in and I ran wildly out the door with a smile as big as the barn door. In less than a minute, I was close enough to jump into her arms. She had kept her promise. She had come back for me!

J. H. JAMES

CHAPTER TWO — NEXT STOP...BOSTON

BACK ON A BUS

My mom and I were back on a bus. This time, we would stay together for a long time to come.

My aunt (stage name "Ginger Lynn") had moved to Boston where she started her show business career. She could tap dance on roller skates, perform acrobatics, and sing. She traveled all over New England and appeared in a wide variety of nightclubs throughout the area.

It was odd that we were now headed to meet up with my aunt in her apartment in the Back Bay of Boston, as the two sisters never really got along that well. I guess it was a matter of "Any port in a storm"!

My mom found a job in the talent agency that represented my aunt. She worked as a clerk typist during the weekdays for a somewhat meager salary.

To supplement her income, Mom worked in the chorus line of the infamous Old Howard Casino in Copley Square in Boston. She would take me with her to work during the evenings when my aunt wasn't available to watch me. I can remember sitting in the dressing room where all the dancers and strippers changed into their costumes. I was only five years old.

J. H. JAMES

OUR FIRST TRAILER

For some reason, unknown to me, my mom and my aunt decided that the Back Bay apartment wasn't a viable fit for them anymore. More than likely, it had to do with the cost of rent in that expensive part of Boston.

They put their heads together and came up with a plan. We would all move into a trailer in Revere, a city that was just eight miles north of Boston and easily accessible by the subway. The trailer was situated in a trailer park, along with approximately a hundred other trailers. The name of the park was Lee's Trailer Park. The monthly rent was $24, including electricity, the trailer, and the lot it sat on.

This was our first trailer. It was 21 feet long and 8 feet wide (one-half the size of our last trailer shown on the cover of this book). It did not have a toilet or running hot water. There was no refrigerator. Instead, it had an icebox. Mr. Wilson, the iceman, would come around every week with large blocks of ice that he carried in the wooden cargo bed in the back of his truck. He would use an ice pick to whittle down the block of ice to the proper size for our small icebox and then use his steel tongs to carry the block inside the trailer where it was placed in a compartment in the center of the icebox with a drip pan underneath it. I can still hear my mom or my aunt yelling at me: "Keep the door closed! You're melting our ice!" The ice had to last an entire week until Mr. Wilson's next visit. He didn't make emergency house calls. Whether our ice lasted the week or not, the iceman did not cometh!

There we were, the three of us, living in a space barely inhabitable for one. My small bed was at the back of the trailer. My mom and my aunt shared the pullout couch in the front of the trailer, which served as their bed.

LEE'S TRAILER PARK

We had no toilet. Instead, there was a porcelain white bucket with a lid that had a handle on it. There was a building with real toilets about a hundred yards from our trailer, which we could access during the day. However, in the middle of a cold Boston winter, when there was an impromptu call of nature in the dark of night, the porcelain bucket was the receptacle of choice. I can still recall the smell of the Lysol we poured inside the bucket as a disinfectant until we could carry it to the toilet building and empty it the following day.

There was no shower or bathtub in our little turtle shell. Mom would heat water on the gas stove and, like a mad chemist, she would mix it with some cold water in the sink in the tiny kitchenette. Hopefully, the temperature would be bearable by the time I sat on the edge of the sink to immerse half of my tiny body into it.

I was always on extra good behavior on bath days! Mom would scrub and rinse my hair in the sink with the pot of water warmed on our small gas stove. I'd hope: *Not too hot, please!* It would be a year later before they installed public showers in the toilet building—still a challenge in the dead of winter.

Speaking of the winter weather, when it became unusually cold (which happened fairly frequently in Boston) our water pipes would freeze. We would have to wait until the trailer park maintenance man could fit us in his queue to eventually come with his blowtorch to thaw out the pipes so we could have running water again. We finally learned about the miracle of wrapping our water pipes with electrical thermal tape at the beginning of our second winter at Lee's. No more frozen pipes!

HOME ALONE

One day, I told my mom I wasn't feeling well and did not want to go to school. She eyed me somewhat suspiciously but opted to let me stay home. We could not afford babysitters or daycare, so there were many times when I was home alone. This was one of them.

The funny thing about playing hooky is that it always seemed like a good idea at the time. However, as the hours passed and boredom set in, I began thinking that maybe it wasn't such a great plan after all. This became even more evident when I could hear the chatter of the other kids in the trailer park returning from school in the afternoon and transitioning into play mode.

Suddenly, I was feeling much better. My feigned sickness magically disappeared. I jumped out of my pajamas and threw on some play clothes so I could join my friends outside.

Much to my surprise, my Aunt Ginger appeared in the middle of the street where we were playing. Apparently, Mom had asked her to stop by and check on me to see if I was OK. When my aunt saw me outside of the trailer, playing with my friends, she immediately launched herself into an angry fit. She walked over and grabbed me by both of my arms. The next thing I knew, she had squatted down and placed me, stomach down, across her lap. She then pulled my pants down in front of all of my friends and gave me a spanking that I will never forget. Then it was back to the trailer for solitary confinement.

When my mom came home from work, I told her what had happened and said that I was sorry for saying that I was sick that morning. She was less interested in my transgression and subsequent apology than she was in my aunt's abhorrent behavior. They ended up having a predictable ballistic confrontation. My aunt packed her things and left the trailer for good. My mom and I were now the only occupants of our humble abode.

Mom did not have a car, so it was the undependable bus or one-foot-in-front-of-the-other that took us to our destinations of choice. Lee's Trailer Park was halfway between Beachmont and Broadway in Revere. The subway train to Boston was located in Beachmont, about two miles east of the trailer park. Broadway was about two miles west in the other direction. That was the area of the city that had shops, restaurants, bars, and the Stop & Shop grocery store.

The buses weren't always on time so, rather than wait for one, we would often just walk to Broadway or Beachmont. The exception was on Fridays when we would either walk or take the bus to the Stop & Shop on Broadway and then take a taxi home with all of our groceries. More on that walking routine later.

MY BLOOD-BROTHER, BOBBY KELLY

As luck would have it, there were a few other kids who lived in "Lee's Trailer Park." (Had there not been any, I could have avoided the embarrassment of my spanking.) One of them was a boy named Bobby Kelly, who quickly became my best friend. In fact, we eventually became blood-brothers. We actually cut our hands and then pressed them together to complete the official blood-brother ceremony—something we had probably picked up on in a movie somewhere along the way. I can't imagine anyone sharing their blood through an open wound in this day and age of AIDS, Covid, and other communicable diseases lurking out there. It would just never happen; but, being carefree and curiously immune children (if we had a cut or a bad bruise we would rub dirt on it to make it better!), we contracted no deathly illness and survived to tell the tale.

Bobby and I agreed that no matter where we went in our lives, we would meet again at the entrance to Lee's Trailer Park when we both turned twenty-one. His birthday was two days earlier than mine. To this very day I still affectionately refer to him as "you old fart!"

Bobby lived in a larger trailer than ours along with his parents and a cocker spaniel named Skippy. Their trailer actually had a bathroom and a small shower. They also owned a car and had another trailer and a speedboat in Laconia, New Hampshire. They would travel to the second trailer on the weekends throughout the summer. It was always a special treat to be invited to Laconia and Lake Winnipesaukee on select summer weekends. I'm certain that it was also a welcome relief for my mom.

Bobby's parents were Mike and Grace. Mike worked at a local papermill, and Grace worked in a diner as a cook. They weren't really well-off by any stretch of the imagination. Their financial status notwithstanding, Bobby was the center of their world and the beneficiary of all of their love, time, attention, money, and most of the material things that he asked for.

I was envious of Bobby Kelly for always seeming to get whatever he wanted from his parents while I was lucky to get some spare change every now and then from my working single mother. I was also envious that he had both a father and mother, something I missed sorely in my life; that was an empty hole, never to be filled in my entire childhood.

SCHOOL DAYS

I would stop by Bobby's trailer every morning, where we would begin our trek off to Wolcott Elementary School. We would walk to school 95% of the time since his dad left for work in the family car very early in the morning. The walk to school was approximately two miles, uphill, via Campbell Avenue through the proverbial snow, rain, sleet, and heat (thankfully, the "gloom of night" was not an issue).

Needless to say, the walk home was a heck of a lot easier at the end of a long school day—downhill all the way. We walked together to school throughout the years, from the first grade, through Garfield Junior High School, and right up to our senior year at Revere High School.

After school in the winter months, there was usually a pick-up game of football. Our football field was a grass-covered median strip pitched at a 45-degree angle. The median separated a set of two-lane highways on which the traffic flowed in opposite directions. Our running plays started out uphill and then cut sharply downhill, allowing the runner to gain speed and momentum. Obviously, running out of bounds was not a good idea! Better to be tackled by one of the defensive players than a 1954 Ford!

All too often, a stray kickoff or an errant pass would find its way to the lower of the two highways. With any luck, an oncoming car would contact the football and send it 30 or 40 yards ahead and off to the side of the highway. When our luck did not hold, the football would end up underneath an approaching vehicle where it met a violent demise in the form of an explosion. When that happened, we did not stick around long enough to see the reaction of the driver of the car. However, something tells me that we were probably responsible for several soiled car seats throughout the years.

Eventually, the day would come when we could ride our bikes to a real football field to play on at Garfield Junior High School. It would feel as though we were going to the Super Dome compared to playing on the slanted and dangerous median, although we would miss the ability to cut sharply downhill on running plays! Until that time would arrive, we were relegated to playing on the median with exploding footballs.

In the warmer months, the pick-up games were baseball instead of football. The baseball field (I use this term very loosely) was located across the street from the infamous football median field. It was in the city dump! We were able to move enough debris and junk to create room for a dirt-covered baseball diamond.

There was a wooden shed behind home plate that had a metal storage cabinet attached to it. We used chalk to draw a box on the metal cabinet to determine strikes and balls. It was "one size fits all," regardless of our height at the plate, although we tried to be as fair as possible with those of us who were vertically challenged. (I was always the smallest of the group.)

When the ball passed home plate, it would make a loud clanging sound as it connected with the metal storage cabinet. It was so annoying that it made better contact hitters of all of us. Even a foul ball was better than hearing the clang of the storage cabinet ringing in our ears. In case you are wondering, we never had enough kids to form teams with a catcher, and thus, the metal cabinet backstop filled that position.

We used what we had to make the game work, and sometimes we were truly resourceful. During one game, we actually used a dead seagull for first base! That definitely motivated us to stretch a single into a double whenever possible. There was no stealing of second base allowed since, once we were on first base, the storage cabinet behind home plate could not throw anyone out at second!

There were thorny bushes along the left side of the diamond. A ball hit in fair territory and bouncing into the bushes became an automatic ground-rule double, saving the fielder from a great deal of unnecessary pain. What a way to learn how to play America's Greatest Pastime.

As it would turn out, this trial by ordeal would serve me well as I later became a fairly decent second baseman who batted first or second in the lineup for the teams I played on. I consistently hit over .330 in camp ball. (No dead seagulls!) I also pitched two no-hitters. More about that summer camp later.

LEE'S TRAILER PARK

OLD TOM

In the building at the trailer park that contained the toilets, and eventually concrete shower stalls, there was also the mailroom. This was approximately a 10-foot by 12-foot room that contained the mail slots for all the incoming mail for trailer park residents. This is where Bobby Kelly and I, and a few of the other kids, would hang out from time to time.

The postman would arrive in the morning to sort out the mail into the pigeonholes bearing the name of the trailers' occupants. We would meet at the mailroom after school to retrieve our mail.

The mailroom was also part of the domain claimed by "Old Tom," who had to be one of the crankiest people ever known to mankind. He was definitely not kid-friendly and would yell at us to move away from the bathhouse or the mailroom on sight. He was the self-appointed sheriff of Lee's Trailer Park. In return for his grumpiness, we would do our best to make his life miserable when he drifted away from his sentry post outside of the bathhouse/mailroom area.

For example, the mailroom also contained a candy machine for public use. Bobby would stand guard outside of the mailroom when Old Tom wasn't around. I would then enter the mailroom and quickly head to the candy machine. It was the type of machine where you would put a nickel in the coin slot and then pull the plunger at the bottom of the row of the candy you wanted. The metal tray the candy was nesting on would collapse and then release the candy bar from behind the glass to the open shelf below.

Since I was the smallest and the skinniest, I was the one most suited for the candy bar caper. It worked best when the candy vendor came to refill the machine by putting the trays back into a horizontal position and then placing the new candy bars on them, making the lower ones more accessible to a kid with a skinny arm. The vendor would fill the machine and then empty the coin box and be on his way.

So . . . the two main pieces of the puzzle that had to be in place were the absence of Old Tom and a fresh refill of the candy bar inventory by the vendor.

When the time was right, Bobby would station himself by the mailroom door to alert me if anyone was coming our way. In a matter of a minute or two, I could slide my skinny arm through the shelf leading to the inside of the candy machine, where I could then reach the bottom rows of the candy bars resting on their little metal racks, awaiting the pull of the plunger to release them. There was no plunger required for me, however. I just reached up and tugged on each metal rack holding a candy bar. I would force it into the down position, releasing the candy bar prisoners held captive in each of the rows. I could only reach about one-third of the way up each row, as that was as far as my small arm would allow me to penetrate. Lots of candy and lots of trips to the dentist for Bobby and me over the course of time.

Eventually, the vending company figured out what was happening and moved to a more sophisticated machine that was arm-proof! Probably just as well, as diabetes would not have been a welcome outcome of our candy capers.

MR. STANLEY THE ICE CREAM MAN

There was a small trailer, perhaps 12 feet long and 8 feet wide, that was located next to the bathhouse building. Outside of the trailer sat an ice cream freezer on wheels. There was a bicycle attached to the back of the freezer. Inside the trailer lived Mr. Stanley, the ice cream man, who was probably pushing his late seventies at the time.

Despite walking with crutches, Mr. Stanley would ride his bicycle/ice cream freezer to a local ice cream distributor and pick up his inventory and some dry ice for the freezer. He would then ride his ice cream bicycle throughout the trailer park and some neighboring streets where he would sell his ice cream.

A popsicle cost ten cents. While that might not seem like much, I seldom had enough money to complete the transaction. Sometimes Mr. Stanley would sell one-half of a broken popsicle for a nickel. I was all-in whenever that opportunity presented itself.

Occasionally, Bobby and I would pool our resources and buy a ten-cent popsicle then split it in half, thereby creating the nickel popsicle through collaboration and cooperation. When you have little in the way of capital, you need to be resourceful to achieve your goals and objectives—something I eventually found to be true throughout my business career.

Somehow, Mr. Stanley made enough money to pay for his trailer rent and his food. Fortunately, he did not need to buy gas for his bicycle! He was quite a guy. Eventually, he succumbed to old age and the nickel popsicle became a thing of the past, like so many other things in life over the years.

EARNING EXTRA MONEY

For me, my call to entrepreneurism came early on in my life, much of it fueled by the need for some spending money, something that we just didn't have much of in those days. As someone once said, "Money isn't everything in life" . . . unless, of course, you run out of it. Then it is everything!

My first encounter with generating revenues occurred when I was just six years old. I had come home from school, changed my clothes, and then began contemplating my first big career move. Mom was at work—home alone again!

I had decided to enter the retail home products sector. First, I would need a product to sell.

J. H. JAMES

After scouring our trailer in search of potential resources, I came across a decent inventory of soap. Evidently, soap was something that my mom felt we should keep an ample supply of. Good for her!

As I recall, I was able to establish an inventory of eight bars of soap. Next, I would have to establish a sales channel and a price point for my products. I settled on a door-to-door sales approach and a price point of five cents per bar (not knowing what price point the market would bear).

My first customer was Trudy (same name as my mom), the waitress who would eventually live in the trailer next door to us. She was often home during the day as she worked mostly nights at Luigi's Italian restaurant in Boston. I knocked on her door and made the pitch. It was a slam dunk! She was in for two bars of soap. My new business was taking off like a rocket!

I spent the next hour knocking on the doors of random trailers. I was able to sell the remaining six bars of soap at a nickel each. Bottom line: forty cents in sales, no overhead, and no inventory issues. Ah, yes! Soap—the sweet smell of success (unless it is being used to wash out your mouth)!

Everything was coming up roses . . . that is until the CEO (Mom) returned home from work. For some strange reason, my mom looked under the sink where the soap had previously been stored and quickly noticed that there were no bars of soap left. To this day, I still wonder if there had been a phone call made from Trudy or another one of my customers to my mom's workplace that day.

After explaining my successful venture to the CEO, she determined that I would need to embark on a product recall initiative. The CEO instructed me to go back to each of my customers and return their money in exchange for the soap that I had sold them. It was embarrassing, disappointing, and a lifelong lesson all wrapped up in one.

LEE'S TRAILER PARK

At the tender age of six, I learned about the importance of integrity in business. While the soap was in our trailer, it wasn't really mine to begin with since my mom had paid for it. Somehow, this little factoid was swept away by my enthusiasm and desire to generate some spending money for myself. Not cool!

Besides my questionable soap selling efforts, there were other ways in which I tried to earn extra spending money. All of us kids owned and collected comic books. After a while, we would have a significant number of comic books in our closets. We would pool our inventories and open a makeshift stand from which we would sell our used comic books.

A new comic book sold for ten cents. We would identify our used comic books by tearing the cover page in half and selling them for five cents. It's not the type of business that went viral, but we were all able to pick up some spare change for one of Mr. Stanley's ice cream cones. Just another day at the office!

I also picked up extra income by delivering groceries from a small, family-owned convenience store near our school. My income stream was formed by tips only!

When we were a little older, Bobby Kelly and I started a trailer wash and wax business. The larger trailers could command a fee of $45.00 for a complete washing and waxing job. The work was arduous and required a sacrifice from any after-school baseball or football games in favor of servicing our clients. The average job took at least two afternoons to complete.

After two or three trailers, we opted to retire in favor of the baseball diamond, which beckoned us from beyond. I had canvassed the entire trailer park and established a card index file of potential customers who wanted our services (some of them were probably previous soap customers!). Rather than just walk away from all of this potential business, we decided to sell our card files to Larry and

Georgie, two brothers who lived in the trailer park and were a few years younger than us. They would take over our customer inventory and then pay us a modest commission as they completed each job. We would be busy focusing on our batting averages.

Unfortunately, it turned out that while Larry and Georgie wanted the business that we had established, they were just a little too young and inexperienced to perform the jobs properly. As I recall, they flooded the trailer of one of their first customers while trying to attach the hose to the sink faucet, which was required for the washing part of the job. This resulted in a call from their mother, Christine, who told us that the boys could not continue on. Another new business bites the dust! It's a jungle out there.

In high school, I met Roy Gross, a new friend, whose father owned a retail egg distribution business. On Saturdays, Roy and I would fill up the back of a station wagon with cartons of eggs for home delivery throughout the Italian section of Revere. His dad paid us for our efforts, and we made a little extra on tips from some of our satisfied customers. I learned that a solid work ethic, a smile, and a friendly attitude are the keys to establishing good relationships and success in sales and service positions, something that seems to be sadly missing in this day and age.

CHAPTER THREE — MOVING ON UP

OUR SECOND TRAILER

I'm uncertain how she managed it, but somehow my mom was able to garner the resources to allow us to move from our first sparse, coffin-like trailer to a larger trailer with a toilet, shower, refrigerator, and hot water! Halleluiah! We were suddenly living in style.

Our second trailer was 32 feet long and 8 feet wide. It had a dining room table that operated on the same principle as a Murphy bed. It folded back into the wall of the trailer for storage, which allowed more space for the living room. When it came time to eat, we unhooked the table and carefully lowered it, allowing a supporting leg to swing out on a hinge from the bottom of the table and rest on the floor. The table was made out of solid oak, and it was very heavy. There was more than one occasion when either my mom or I became a victim of the table slipping from our grip and making contact with our heads— possibly another event leading to my having to write it down when I have more than two items on my grocery list!

My new bedroom was bigger than my old one, and there was a larger couch in the front of the trailer that had a pullout bed, which Mom no longer had to share with her sister. Later on, however, she would be sharing it with someone else.

Our second trailer was on a different lot, thereby giving us new neighbors. On one side of us lived Trudy (the single waitress who was a prior VIP soap customer). On the other side of us was a similarly sized trailer as ours that was home to Christine, Larry, and Georgie.

Christine was a divorced, single working mother just like my mom. In those days, there was a stigma attached to being a single, divorced mother, so my mom and Christine quickly became comrades in arms as they worked hard to provide for their children and to make their way in the world. Occasionally, they would go out together to one of the bars at Revere Beach to break loose and have some fun when their funds would allow it, which was fairly infrequently (realizing, of course, that they usually would not have to pay for all of their drinks themselves).

Christine was not much of a drinker, unlike my mom, who came from a family of hard-hitting drinkers and who also had experience working in nightclubs in New York City when she was younger. In other words, my mom could handle her liquor much better than Christine could. Inevitably, when the two of them went out to party, Christine would end up physically sick, and my mom would have to shepherd her home to safety. They were definitely an Oscar and Felix combination but remained close friends for many, many years.

Christine's two children were the boys who took over Bobby's and my ill-fated trailer wash 'n' wax business. While Georgie was the oldest of the two, he had developmental issues that would stunt his emotional growth throughout his lifetime. He would never become more than fifteen or sixteen years old mentally. Georgie's younger brother, Larry, was a few years younger than Bobby and me. His mental faculties were in good order, and he would end up having a full life with a good job and a wife and children at some point in his future.

While Bobby and I were the movers and shakers of our own little world within the neighborhood, we sometimes allowed Larry and

LEE'S TRAILER PARK

Georgie to join in on our activities. Some of this was out of necessity since there weren't always enough kids to field even a shorthanded baseball or football team. We were often recruiting kids from other nearby neighborhoods to get the numbers we needed to play sports. When push came to shove, Larry and Georgie were always available to play "Cowboys and Indians," tag, kick-the-can, hide & seek, giant steps, or army games.

Speaking of games, Bobby and I each had bows and arrows. For some inexplicable reason, Bobby and I decided that a fun game would be for the two of us to stand back-to-back and shoot our arrows straight up in the air while Larry and Georgie (and a few other misguided kids) would run out into the field while trying to avoid the downward flight of the arrows.

In somewhat of a weak attempt at defending our obvious lack of good judgment, the arrows had target tips that were round and not used for hunting. Admittedly, that fact would be academic if one in our group of arrow runners had caught an arrow in the eye. During one of our bow-and-arrow sessions, Bobby was feathering his arrow in his bow when he accidentally released it before aiming all the way to the sky. The unintended target became Georgie, who gaped in horror as the arrow hit him in the chest and then mercifully bounced off to the ground. That was our last "bow and arrow—run for your life game" ever!

THE CREEK AND THE REEDS

Behind the infamous bathhouse building sat a large field of reeds, which grew next to Chelsea Creek. In the summer, the reeds would grow to a height of six feet or more. One of our favorite pastimes was to walk through the reeds and create secret paths. We would also find places where we could stamp down the reeds and build imaginary campsites. This made for great army games and hide & seek adventures.

As the summer waned, the reeds would become dry and rigid, thereby making them perfect spears in our war games. At least we didn't use our bows and arrows! However, I'm uncertain that, in all honesty, we could consider this a safety upgrade of any real magnitude.

The reeds provided us with anonymity and a blank screen for our imaginations to run wild. It was a perfect make-believe world that we could quickly slip into from time to time. We just had to be on the lookout for an unwelcome snake (most of them were green and harmless) or a wayward rat from the nearby garbage dump at the bathhouse building.

With the onset of fall, the reeds would become brown and brittle. For some strange reason, they seemed to catch on fire every year. Our gang would dutifully watch the firemen as they put out the fire after much of the field had already burned to the ground (much to the delight of nearby residents of the trailer park and homes in the area who secretly thought of us as heroes).

We could hear the rats shrieking as the reeds burned down to the ground and into some of their burrowing holes. Innocent as newborn babes, we were just passing the time as the flames reached up into the sky. Oh well; there weren't enough kids to field a sports team on those fire days anyway, so we had to find something to keep us occupied!

Chelsea Creek ran parallel to the weeds. It was like a living, breathing organism that came from an alien planet. It contained oil, sludge, fuel, trash, some water, and probably an unknown amount of sewage. The creek was part of the tidal pool that was influenced by the nearby Atlantic Ocean. On some days it would be extremely low, and on other days it would rise to a level that our homemade rafts could navigate.

When the creek level was high enough, we would go fishing for minnows. (The thought that there was actually life in that creek now sends chills up my spine.) We would take empty milk bottles and partially fill them with breadcrumbs. Then, we would tie a string around the top of each of the milk bottles and throw the bottles out into the deeper water. Lo-and-behold! Minnows would swim into the milk bottles to nibble on the bread.

All we had to do was pull on the string to remove the bottles and the minnows from the creek. Oddly enough, there was no endgame here. It's not like we started a campfire and cooked the minnows (thank God). Nor did we use them for bait because there were no bigger fish in the creek. (None of the minnows would make it to full fish size for obvious reasons.) We ended up releasing them back into the creek, perhaps to make their way back into our milk bottles on a future fishing expedition.

Another creek adventure was rafting. We would pull two discarded wooden pallets from the creek bed and place one of them with the flat side on the water and the other across the bottom one with the flat side up. We cut some sturdy branches for steering poles and then headed out into the creek. Bobby and I were like Tom Sawyer and Huckleberry Finn on steroids!

Bobby's father, Mike, told us stories of kids drowning in Chelsea Creek when he was younger. I'm uncertain if they were true; however, I am confident that he did not want us messing around in that creek. Anyway, other than some missteps into the oily sludge that sometimes came up to our knees, we made it out alive. There was no hiding where we had been when our parents saw our filthy, slimy clothes when we arrived home. Caught red-handed every time!

J. H. JAMES

THE OIL TANKS

On the other side of the stream, where the creek funneled into oblivion, sat Suffolk Downs Racetrack and a huge oil farm with large cylindrical tanks storing oil and gas for future use. The tanks were surrounded by six-foot-high fences with chicken wire running along the top. A moat of collected rainwater (and God only knows what else) also encircled each tank. Obviously, the goal was to keep out unwanted intruders.

During the wintertime, the water in the moats would turn to ice, thereby creating a series of natural ice ponds protected from the wind by the tanks themselves. Bingo! Instant hockey rinks!

We would grab our skates, cross the stream at the end of the creek, and stealthily head for the fencing around the tanks. Since we could not scale the fences, the obvious way to breach this barrier was to dig underneath them. We would hollow out the ground underneath the fences and then pull back on the bottom of them to create a gap for entry. Anywhere from eight to ten of us would meet at a designated fence location on a given day and time.

Once inside the perimeter of the fence, we would create hockey goals with rocks and sticks near the tanks. Then it was time to lace up our skates and let the games begin. While there was little in the way of a manned security operation back in those days, there were some huts and small offices in the inner sanctum of the tanks where staff members were on duty drinking coffee and staying warm.

Everything would go along just fine . . . that is until an errant hockey puck would hit one of the almost-empty oil tanks. This created a loud gong-like sound that was crushing to the ear. It also served as an alert to those working in the offices and huts that an intrusion had occurred.

We could hear them coming toward us and yelling for us to stop. Then it was off with the skates, hockey sticks in hands, and a mad dash for the fence. We were never physically caught but had too many close calls to count. Each new hockey event meant selecting a different tank pond and a new entrance under the fence, hoping we would not be discovered again.

On the way home, and a safe distance from the tanks, there was a small diner just before we reached the creek bed. There was a very nice elderly lady who worked at the counter (I think her name was Margaret) who thought the world of my blood-brother, Bobby. Maybe it was because Bobby's mother also worked at a diner or perhaps it was because Bobby had a million-dollar smile and a gentle attitude (unlike me). I'm thinking it was the latter of the two reasons.

Anyway, we would enter the diner, place our skates and sticks in a corner, and then hop on two of the round stools in front of the counter. Margaret would dutifully give each of us a free piece of apple pie and a cup of hot chocolate. She was an angel. Nothing could be better after a mad dash from the oil tanks than hot chocolate and warm apple pie. Thanks, Bobby, for letting me trail in your wake.

THE RAILROAD YARD

Immediately adjacent to Lee's Trailer Park was the American Legion Highway, six lanes of never-ending traffic separated by a narrow dirt-and-grass median. On the other side of the highway was a large railroad yard just perfect for discovery and adventure. There were also main tracks surrounding the yard on which freight trains would occasionally speed by on their way to their next destination.

Once crossing the main tracks we were in a new world of our own. Empty, abandoned box cars, each one ready for exploring, providing endless inspiration for our imaginations to wander. While exciting, we were always on the lookout for any hoboes that might be lurking in the empty boxcars or straggling nearby. Fortunately, we never encountered any, assuming, of course, that they were even there to begin with.

On our way back from the railroad yard, we would sometimes stop to place pennies on a train track and wait it out until the next freight train sped by. One of the first things we learned is that it is not a good idea to be too close to the tracks when the trains fly by as they create a vacuum that pulls you toward the passing train and the tracks. Once we had the pennies on the track, we would retreat from the tracks to a safe distance where we would wait for an oncoming train.

Now for the fun! After the train passed, we would head down to the tracks where we had placed our pennies. The round pennies were now oblong and had magically grown to the size of silver dollars. I do not remember where we learned about this phenomenon, only that it provided some adventure, fun, and fascination for us.

THE FIRE AT CHRISTINE'S TRAILER

When it snowed heavily during the wintertime, school would be canceled, and playtime was the order of the day. We would build igloos on the opposite sides of one of the small streets running through the trailer park. Following the completion of the igloo construction was a serious snowball fight, which usually ended because of our sheer exhaustion or because one of us took a solid snowball to the face. (There's that safety issue raising its ugly head again.)

When we were a little older, snow also presented Bobby and me with the opportunity to make a few extra bucks by shoveling out walkways and driveways for residents who were desperate to escape the confines of their trailers. During a decent storm, we could net as much as $12 to $15 each, which was always a welcome revenue stream. Hard work but well worth it as far as we were concerned.

LEE'S TRAILER PARK

One day, after finishing our snow shoveling, we were heading back to my trailer. Suddenly, we heard cries for help coming from Christine's trailer next door. Bobby and I ran over and noticed that smoke was billowing out from the inside of the trailer. Larry and Georgie were inside.

Bobby and I quickly ran up to the front door where we could clearly see the cause of the fire. Larry and Georgie had been out playing in the snow. When they returned to their trailer, they placed their wet clothes on top of the small oil furnace that provided the much-needed heat for the trailer in cold weather. Apparently, they neglected to check on their clothes periodically and turn them over to the other side. The clothes were on fire and the rest of the trailer was definitely next in the fire's pecking order.

Bobby dashed deeper into the trailer, grabbed Larry and Georgie, and led them through the smoke to the safety of the front door. I somehow was able to quickly remove the burning clothes and throw them out into the snow in one fell swoop. It was a miracle that I wasn't burned and that no one was hurt during this crisis. Our moms would learn about what happened after they returned home from work later in the day.

Bobby and I both received commendations from our Boy Scout Troop for our quick and decisive action. There was no CNN in those days, so the accolades ended with the awarding of a ribbon to each of us at our next troop meeting with our parents in tow.

Anyway, we were happy that everything ended up as it did with no one getting injured and Christine's trailer remaining intact. Everything could have turned out a lot worse had Bobby and I not just happened by at the right time.

J. H. JAMES

SNOWBALLS AND BUSES

Speaking of snow . . . Bobby and I were walking home from school during the dead of winter. We had been hit with about four to five inches of snow during the morning, but, unfortunately, not enough to cancel school for the day.

When it snowed, one of our favorite mischievous pastimes was to throw snowballs at the buses as they passed by. Other than startling the occasional unsuspecting passenger when the snowball contacted a bus window (which admittedly was the intent of our mission), this was a harmless exercise not meant to cause damage to property or people.

During one of our snowball-throwing episodes, a Revere Police Cruiser appeared seemingly out of nowhere with lights flashing and the siren blaring. The two police officers stopped their cruiser in front of us and then motioned us over to join them in a little conversation! The driver rolled down his window and asked us, "What do you boys think you're doing?"

To which we replied (almost in unison), "Just walking home from school."

The officer responded, "Does 'just walking home from school' include throwing snowballs at the buses going by?"

Before either of us could summon up an answer he looked me squarely in the eye and said, "What is your name?" Uh-oh!

"My name is Jesse James," I replied.

"You're a regular little wise guy aren't you? Let me ask you again, what is your name?"

I repeated, "Jesse James." He then opened the door of the cruiser and stepped out. An extra change of underwear would have been welcome at this point.

He looked over at Bobby, while pointing toward me, and said, "What is his name?"

LEE'S TRAILER PARK

Bobby said, "His name is Jesse James. Honest, sir. That is his real name."

"What is your name?" Bobby paused for a second and then said, "My name is Bobby Kelly and we both live at Lee's Trailer Park." The old saying is to never offer information unless they ask you to. Anyway, Bobby thought that it was important to let him know where we lived.

I guess that the officer concluded that he and his partner had served their purpose by scaring the hell out of us when they pulled over to confront us. He must have also concluded that Jesse James was, in fact, my real name. He looked at both of us sternly and said, "You boys better be on your way home. Right now! And no more throwing snowballs at the buses. Got it?"

"Yes, sir," we responded in unison.

"OK . . . on your way then."

To this very day, Bobby tells me that when the cop asked him what his name was that he paused and was about to say, "Frank James" (the real Jesse James's brother's name) but he chickened out and played it straight. Probably lucky for us that he did, or we would have been sitting inside of the police car in a matter of seconds. My name is a door opener, but sometimes it can be an annoyance as well.

MARY MILLER

Mary Miller's trailer was located a block from ours. She was in her seventies and lived with her husband, Joe, who was closer to eighty. Mary was the sweetest, kindest woman I had ever known in my young life and for many years to follow. I think she may have been related to Mother Teresa—at least it seemed so.

Her husband was more of a grump, which I imagine was a product of his advancing years and declining health. He eventually passed on, leaving Mary Miller to make it to the finish line on her own.

J. H. JAMES

Mary was a devout Catholic and tried to never miss a Sunday Mass or Communion. Since Mom was still without a car, I would ride to church on Sundays with Mary Miller. I also helped her with chores in her trailer and yard work from time to time.

Mom wasn't much for going to church, and she was pretty tired from working two jobs by the time Sunday rolled around. While I went to church with Mary Miller, Mom slept in.

There were those occasional times when Mary wasn't able to make it to Mass, in which case I walked the mile and a half to church on my own. No worries. This gave me the opportunity to leave church a little early and get a head-start home in time for the Sunday football games.

Anyway, it was on a Halloween evening when my mom and I went next door to Christine's trailer, after trick-or-treating ended, to visit with her and Larry and Georgie. While we were there, a few Halloween stragglers knocked on Christine's door looking for treats.

Just as the trick-or-treat dust had settled, there was another knock on the trailer door. When Christine opened the door, with a treat in hand, we all saw an old man standing in front of the doorstep. He never said a word . . . just stood there, sort of hunched over and motionless.

Christine and my mom asked him who he was but there was no response. He looked somewhat sad, despondent, and remained silent. Finally, Christine opened the door wide and asked him if he wanted to come in and have some tea! He never replied but just entered the trailer and sat himself down on the small couch at the front of the tiny living room.

As the tea was steeping, Larry, Georgie, and I joined in on the interrogation of the old stranger. "Who are you? Where are you from? Why are you here?" No answer.

Finally, as the tea was being served, the old man broke into a smile. Then . . . suddenly . . . a high-pitched voice said, "You mean, you don't know who I am?"

We were all in shock when we realized that the old man sitting on the couch was none other than—yes—Mary Miller! She had painstakingly made herself up to look like an old man on Halloween. Never in a million years would we have thought that the kind, sweet, quiet, church-going Mary Miller could pull off a Halloween caper like this one. We were all roaring with laughter as Mary removed her wig, makeup, and bifocals to reveal the perpetrator of this Halloween joke. My rides to church with Mary Miller would never be the same!

LITTLE EVEL KNIEVEL

There was a nice-sized hill leading down into Lee's Trailer Park from the highway that skirted the perimeter of the park. In the wintertime, it made for great sled riding and snow coaster riding (round aluminum coasters that we would sit on and go around in circles when we coasted downhill out of control).

In the summer, the hill served as a launching pad in which we could build up considerable speed on our bicycles before entering the series of streets that formed the grid inside the trailer park. Either Old Tom or nasty Walter (the park owner and Mrs. Lee's second husband) was constantly yelling at us to slow down. "No fast bike riding allowed in the park!"

One day, I was speeding down the hill when I took a sharp left turn onto Second Street (aptly named as it was the street after the first street in the park) and headed toward the mailroom building. Much to my surprise and distress, as I approached the intersection at the front of the building, there was a car coming up the street perpendicular to my right-hand side. My bike and the car were doomed to collide.

J. H. JAMES

I hit the brakes on the bike with all my might, which resulted in an uncontrollable skid on the sandy surface of the old blacktopped road. My bike came crashing to the ground and slid forward on its side with me still gripping the handlebars in fear. The car coming up the street also hit its brakes as it entered the intersection and skidded as well.

Miracle of miracles . . . the car came to a complete stop just as my bike and I slid beneath it and also came to a complete stop. I finally opened my eyes and looked up at the underside of the car. I was still alive and did not have a scratch on me! I heard Old Tom when he started hollering at me about riding too fast in the park as he pulled me and my bike out from underneath the car.

My days of speeding through the trailer park on my bicycle had come to an abrupt end. From now on, it was "safety first." No more stunt riding! Lesson learned.

WHEW! That was a close one . . . actually, it was only one of three times in my childhood when I flirted with serious injury or death and escaped unscathed.

CHAPTER FOUR — ENTER TONY

HITCHHIKING

Mom's system for managing her monthly budget consisted of several 3x5 manila envelopes stored in a small box with a flip-down lid. Each envelope had the type of expense it represented in her budget written on the face of the envelope: rent, electric, gas, telephone, groceries, transportation, etc.

Since they paid Mom on a weekly basis, she would dutifully place the portion of cash required to get us through the month in each envelope. She based the math for the system on four weeks in a month. As luck would have it, there were five paydays in a month four times a year. This resulted in our having extra cash available at the end of those months.

We usually celebrated by taking the subway to Chinatown in Boston for a fabulous Chinese dinner at Gamsum's Restaurant (now long gone). Mom taught me how to order dinner for the two of us and would allow me to have the honors when our server arrived at the table. We always ordered egg rolls, chicken chow mein, and lobster Cantonese-style. There was never a morsel of food remaining to be boxed up and taken home.

J. H. JAMES

On one of those extra paycheck occasions, we walked from Lee's Trailer Park to the subway station at Beachmont. Next stop, downtown Boston and Chinatown!

I was six years old at the time and had become quite the clown (and an occasional nuisance). We were about halfway into our two-mile trek when I stepped off the sidewalk and stuck my thumb out like a hitchhiker. Mom scolded me and told me to return to the sidewalk. I just chuckled and kept my thumb waving in the wind as cars flew by. Suddenly, and much to my surprise and horror, a brand-new gray Oldsmobile began to slow down and then stopped shortly ahead of us.

There were two men in the car. When we walked up even with the car, the passenger window slid down and the driver leaned across and asked, "Do you need a lift?" Mom quickly told him that we were only going as far as the subway at Beachmont and that we were almost there. The man said, "No problem. We would be happy to drive you the rest of the way."

For some unknown reason, Mom decided to trust the good-looking man behind the wheel. She opened the back door and we climbed in. (Watch your fingers, Mom!)

During the brief ride to the subway, the man introduced himself as Tony and his friend in the passenger seat as Al. In the short time that it took for us to reach our destination, Tony had successfully obtained our telephone number from my mom.

They would begin dating, and Tony would eventually become my stepfather (sort of). Our lives would change profoundly forever because I waved my small thumb at passing cars while walking with my mom to the subway. You can't make this stuff up.

Despite his initial politeness in offering to drive us to the subway station, I found Tony to be gruff and somewhat scary. I was definitely afraid of him.

The good news for me was that he was in the aluminum siding business, which caused him to travel away from home on a fairly extensive basis. All that I knew was that he and Mom were dating and sleeping together in our trailer when he was in town.

Tony told Mom that he had been married before but was now divorced. He said that he had two children from that marriage. In fact, during one of my birthday parties, he brought his two children as guests. The oldest was a boy who was eight years old at the time. His sister was six years old, and I was just turning seven. They seemed nice enough, despite my misgivings about their father. The extra presents helped us to bond!

THE INTERVENTION AND REVELATION

It's fair to say that I was somewhat of a rambunctious and rebellious kid. My mom and I were like oil and water at times. We just didn't mix well together. It would be many years down the road before I became familiar with the term "acting out" as it relates to bad behavior by children (and my attitude in particular).

Apparently, I had pushed her to the edge of her tolerance level one day, and she decided to take action. As I recall, I came home from school (fifth grade at the time) and was surprised to see both my mom and Tony sitting on the couch. It was extremely rare for him to be around during the day (and many nights as well). Although I sort of accepted Tony as just her boyfriend, I was extremely leery of him. He was of Italian heritage and proudly displayed all the attributes of a typical "Boston wiseguy."

I noticed that there were butterflies in my stomach, and they weren't flying in formation. My anxiety was taken to the next level when my mom looked over at me and said, "I'm going next door to see Christine. Tony wants to talk to you." Not a good omen!

J. H. JAMES

Tony had a bad leg. He said he was wounded in the war and was saved by a medical service dog—a story that would later prove to be false. Actually, the bad leg resulted from polio that he had when he was younger. Anyway, he wore a heavy metal brace on his left leg and carried a cane. He was also very strong and could be extremely aggressive toward me when he chose to be. No sooner had the door closed behind my mom (watch your fingers, Mom!) when Tony clicked his brace in place and stood. He looked at me and said, "Follow me." Not good!

We walked to my small bedroom, which was at the back of the trailer. As we made the short trip from the front to the back, Tony would stop at each jalousie window and crank it closed. Really, really not good, for certain!

When we made it to my bed, he sat down beside me and began to berate me for my bad behavior and for not getting along better with my mom. I hoped that this would be one of those "sticks and stones" moments where the words really couldn't hurt me, as scary and threatening as they were. Out of nowhere, his right hand came up and then out in a downward motion where it landed on my face. He continued to "teach me a lesson" for the next three or four minutes. I tried my best to protect myself, but it was a fruitless effort.

When both the attack and my crying ended, Tony opened all the windows on his journey back to the couch at the front of the trailer. My mom returned a short while afterward, smoking a cigarette and not offering much in the way of conversation. I was still silently sobbing while my body was shaking uncontrollably.

The next morning, I awoke, dressed, and headed off to school.

Once in class, after reciting the Lord's Prayer (yes, we prayed together, even in public school, back in those days) and the Pledge of Allegiance, my teacher called me to her desk. She asked, "Are you OK?"

My reluctance to answer right away prompted her to take me out into the hallway where we could have more privacy.

Apparently, some of the blows I had received the previous day resulted in some swelling on my face and forehead. I was uncertain whether to make up a story or to just blurt out the truth. I settled for what I believed to be the truth, perhaps thinking it might be a way to strike back at Tony.

I told my teacher that my mother was upset at me and had asked "a male friend of hers" to beat me back into order. It is important to note here that, as far as I was concerned, Tony was my mom's boyfriend at that time. No one had ever told me otherwise. Tony and my mom had been "seeing each other" for more than three years at this point in their relationship.

My sharing of the events of the previous day with my teacher resulted in her calling my mom into the school for a meeting. After the meeting, my mom told me that she and Tony had been married for some time. He wasn't just "a friend" who had punished me; he was my stepfather that had punished me. She further explained that she'd told the teacher that the swelling on my face resulted from my trying to protect myself and that my own hands and arms had inflicted the damage (known as "defensive wounds" as I would learn later on in life).

So, that was it. Case closed! I had a new stepfather who I never knew was anything more than just my mom's long-time boyfriend. I recovered from the swelling on my face and life moved on. Still, I found myself wishing that I had been born without thumbs!

TAKE THE GOOD WITH THE BAD

Every day that Tony traveled was like a holiday for me. I never did (nor will I ever) understand what my mom saw in Tony other than his nice new cars and his money. He would drive up to the front of the trailer with a brand-new Cadillac convertible every year. His gambling and philandering would only get worse as the years went on, but she would never deny her love for him. I guess that love, like beauty, is in the eye of the beholder.

I feel obligated to point out that while there were definitely some very dark moments in my relationship with Tony, it was not all doom and gloom. It's interesting how the human spirit can often find the best in even the worst situations.

I would occasionally get to go with Tony and my mom to the drive-in movies. For the uninitiated, a drive-in movie consisted of rows and rows of cars parked next to poles with speakers that would be placed inside each car to provide sound for the movie that was being shown on a giant screen in front of the first row. There were also electric heaters provided on the speaker poles that could be pulled inside the car during cold weather to avoid having to run the engine and use gas during the movies. With as many as a hundred or so cars on the theater lot, all those running engines would have generated too much white noise to compete with the movie sound—and all those idling motors could have easily resulted in asphyxiation from carbon monoxide poisoning for patrons enjoying the show. So, the heaters and speakers were an essential part of the movie-viewing experience.

There was also the obligatory playground that kids could frolic in before darkness and the start of the movie. There were swing sets, merry-go-rounds, and slides to while away the time until the dark captured the night.

I was always assigned the task of going to the refreshment stand during the intermission to load up on goodies for the three of us. It was a chore that I actually enjoyed.

In addition to the drive-in movies, I was also occasionally invited to dinner at some of the great Italian restaurants in Boston when Tony and my mom went out on the town. The one that we frequented the most was Polcari's in the North End. Great food, great ambiance, and great service!

Tony was a gambler and loved to play cards—the latter actually being a skill of his I enjoyed learning. Even at the tender age of seven, I was a very accomplished card player. We played gin rummy on the weekends. Through the years, I beat him many more times than I lost to him. He was not a very good loser.

On some weekends, Tony and I would go to a nearby pool hall on Saturday morning. He would give me my allowance and then promptly take it back from me over the pool table. He beat me (no pun intended) many more times than I beat him. I think that subconsciously I did not really mind losing (not a good outlook to have in life) as long as I was able to spend time with him, as, sadly, he was the closest thing I would ever have to a real father. I guess it was another case of "any port in a storm."

MOM'S NEW JOB

Mom worked her way up and out of her clerk-typist job at the talent agency and was no longer dancing at the Old Howard Casino in Scully Square. She ended up working for the US government as a clerk typist with a grade level of GS-2.

Mom did not even have a high school education, as she left her home at age sixteen and never had the opportunity to pursue her studies and get her diploma. She was too busy working to support us to have time for studies. That would come later in life. She was fortunate to land her new job at the U.S. Naval Hospital in Chelsea, Massachusetts, which is next to Revere. She now had a full-time job with vacation, sick leave, benefits, and some stability in her life.

It would take some years, but Mom would pass her GED and finally have her diploma. She would eventually become a purchasing agent and attain a grade of GS-13 prior to her disability retirement after many years of working in the government. Besides Chelsea Naval Hospital, she worked for NASA and the Department of Labor.

Mom was a shining example of what one can achieve with a strong work ethic and a commitment to excellence. One day, we had a "wikked baad Baastan" winter snowstorm. Over twelve inches of snow had fallen overnight and continued to fall throughout the morning.

The buses weren't running, and the telephone service was out. Dutifully devoted, Mom bundled up and began the trek through the snow from our trailer in Revere to the Chelsea Naval Hospital. She walked through the deep snow and the driving wind for more than eight miles to reach the hospital and her desk. Once there, she discovered that they had closed the administrative facilities because of the storm. Mercifully, someone recognized what she had gone through to make it to work and had arranged to have her driven back home.

From elevator operator and cigarette girl to dancing at the Old Howard Casino to a high-level position in the US government with a significant pension . . . not too bad! Thanks for setting an example of a solid work ethic and commitment for me to follow later on in life. Way to go, Mom!

CHAPTER FIVE- CAMP ROTARY

SUMMER AT LEE'S TRAILER PARK

Once school came to a close for the summer, many of the kids in the neighborhood went on vacations, which meant that there were times when there was no one to play with. It also presented a challenge in terms of who would watch me all summer long. Leave it to Tony to come up with a solution to this problem.

Evidently, Tony was a "connected guy" when it came to getting things done. He apparently had a friend who lived in Lynn, Massachusetts (the next city just north of Revere), who was involved with a summer camp called Camp Rotary in Boxford, Massachusetts.

The camp was an overnight summer camp funded by the Rotary Club of Lynn and other benefactors as well. It was for boys from age of eight to sixteen. For the record, I was still only six years old at the time.

Tony worked his usual magic and pulled a few strings to allow me to enroll in the camp at age six instead of age eight. Not only did this solve the dilemma of who would watch over me during the summer days, but it also gave Tony and my mom the freedom to spend more time together while I was away at camp.

J. H. JAMES

When Mom approached me with the idea of attending camp, I immediately said, "Yes." I had (and still have) a fairly resilient and adventurous nature about me. Besides, anything had to be better than spending long hot summers in Lee's Trailer Park with no one to hang out with except Larry and Georgie. Bobby and his parents were gone most of the summer, spending their weekends at their trailer and their boat on Lake Winnipesaukee.

The idea was to enroll me for only two weeks for the first year to see how I liked it. I was "all-in."

OFF TO CAMP

When I arrived at Camp Rotary, not only was I already two years younger than many of the other first-year campers but I was also always the smallest boy in my group, same as in my classes at school. You could always find me in a group photo by looking at the last person either on the left or the right end of the first row.

What I lacked in size I made up for with heart and effort. I excelled in baseball, swimming, badminton, track, sharpshooting, and most other activities as well (although learning how to swim would eventually prove to be a huge challenge for me).

I took to my first two weeks at Camp Rotary like it was my home away from home. When Tony and my Mom came to take me home at the end of the two weeks, the first words out of my mouth were, "Can I stay another two weeks?"

While Tony couldn't work his magic that first year since the camp was fully booked for the summer, I would become the perennial two-month camper for the next eight years. One of my last two years there I served as a junior counselor and the other year I worked on the maintenance staff, thereby avoiding the weekly enrollment fees, which was a plus for Mom and Tony.

Now, back to my swimming challenge. Our designated swim area was located on Styles Pond, directly adjacent to the camp. Two elongated piers extended from the lake shore out into the lake. The distance between the piers was approximately twenty-five yards. The first ten yards of shallow water were lined off by a rope of buoys attached to the two piers.

In order to swim in the deeper water on the outside of the rope line, we needed to pass our swim test, which would result in graduating from a "Minnow" designation (when catching minnows in the creek, I never knew that I would become one!) to a "Fish" designation. That test consisted of swimming the entire twenty-five yards from pier to pier on the deep side of the rope line.

For some reason, I had an innate fear of the deep water and was content to be confined to the Minnow section of the swim area for the first two years I was at Camp Rotary. My counselors, junior counselors, and friends encouraged me to "take the plunge" and pass my test by swimming the twenty-five yards on the outside of the rope line, but I was petrified and would have no part of it. The strange thing is, I could swim the twenty-five yards on the inside of the line without any problem at all!

In my third year at Camp Rotary, I befriended a junior counselor called "Jumbo." As you might imagine, he was a big boy with a rather rotund build. He was also the salt of the earth and was liked by everyone who knew him.

One day, Jumbo told me that if I would swim the twenty-five yards outside of the rope line to pass my swim test, he would swim beside me to make certain that I was completely safe during my effort to succeed. I trusted him and liked him, so I took him up on his offer. The day finally arrived when Jumbo and I swam together on the outside of the rope line. I officially became a Fish. I was both happy and proud beyond belief!

One of the ironies of passing the swim test was realizing how fear had stopped me from achieving my goal even though the fear was propagated by one thin rope line. Obviously, the depth of the water on one side of the line versus the other was insignificant. It was the space between my ears that was holding me back (a lesson that would remain with me throughout my life). Thanks to Jumbo, I was able to overcome my fear. Not only that, but I had fallen in love with swimming (deep water notwithstanding) from that point forward.

I ended up joining the swim team and set several records in swimming. I was also the lead swimmer on our team, which remained undefeated for the six consecutive years I was on it. To put things in their proper perspective, I was a very good swimmer but not destined to be the next Mark Spitz.

This was a camp swim team that competed against other camps in New England. I hadn't the style, size, or stroke to compete at an Olympic level or anything close to it. When the starter's pistol was fired it looked like someone had thrown an outboard motor into the water when I dove into it. Nothing but wild splashing and the unbridled flailing of strokes as fast as I could move . . . yet, somehow, I continued to finish in first place again and again.

I learned that "If you feed your fear, your faith will die. If you feed your faith, your fear will die." Those two emotions cannot occupy the same space at the same time.

A DOGGONE TOUGH DECISION

I remember waking up on a Saturday morning in our trailer between camp seasons. I heard what sounded like a whining noise coming from our living room. I ambled out of my bedroom and discovered a small brown and white puppy in a box near the kitchen. I picked him up and held him close to my chest and almost melted into his paws.

The puppy and I played for a while until Tony and Mom woke up and joined in the festivities. Naturally, I wanted to keep the puppy for my own. Tony explained that the only way I could have the puppy was if I would give up going to Camp Rotary during the summers so that I could take care of the puppy properly.

Even at the tender age of eight, I remember thinking, Why did Tony bring the puppy home in the first place? I concluded that he knew that I would not give up my summers at Camp Rotary no matter how much I wanted the puppy. Tough choice. I elected to continue going to Camp Rotary instead of having my summers alone in Lee's Trailer Park with the puppy. The reason for, and the destiny of, the puppy would become clear in a number of years. I learned that the best decisions are not always the easiest to make.

Back at camp, Sundays were always visiting days at Camp Rotary. The gates would open at one o'clock p.m., immediately following lunch. The road from the main gate to the campus was well over a mile long. After lunch, I would run the length of the road and sit on a stone wall near the gate waiting to see Tony and my mom arrive for their weekly visit. The other kids would just stay at the campus and wait for their parents there. Apparently, while a resilient kid, I was also somewhat needy and always eager to see Mom (not so much Tony) on Sundays.

Every now and then, Mom and Tony had something else on their agenda and weren't able to visit me on Sunday. For some unknown reason, the communications were not very clear on those weeks, and I did not always realize that they were not coming to visit until I was waiting at the gate for them and they didn't show up. I would wait and wait but eventually took the long walk back from the gate to the main campus disheartened and forlorn.

On the other side of the coin, Mom and Tony would show up on their visiting days with a watermelon to share with my cabinmates during Sunday dinner. This became a visiting day fad with other parents bringing watermelons to their kids on Sundays. The camp eventually had to stop parents from bringing watermelons as it became labor-intensive for the kitchen to store all of them in the walk-in refrigerator and cut them up during dinner. Fun while it lasted though!

Also, Mom would sometimes mail me a tin of Barricini candies. That helped to make me an instant hero with my fellow campers in our cabin. What Mom and Tony lacked in the way of consistency of Sunday visits they tried to make up with some special gifts from time to time. In my mind, the candy equated to a display of love. Yes, I could be bought for the right price!

I eventually figured it out. My going to camp was a plus for Mom and Tony, who had most of the summer and some of their weekends to themselves. One year, they even drove from Boston to Las Vegas where they stayed and played for two weeks at the Flamingo Hotel.

The good news is that I loved going to camp and felt that the tradeoff was worth it. Not much to do at Lee's Trailer Park in the summer anyway.

THE FISH DEN

As I mentioned, there were three times in my young life that I escaped from the Grim Reaper. The first was the time that my bicycle slid underneath a car at the trailer park.

The second time occurred at Camp Rotary. As an accomplished swimmer, I finally worked my way up to becoming a lifeguard during our afternoon swim times.

One of the perks of being a lifeguard is that you were able to change from your clothes into your bathing suit in an area beneath the dining hall (actually the building's foundation), which was immediately next to Styles Pond and our swim area. This saved time for the lifeguards by not having to go all the way back to their cabins (a healthy hike) to change. It also allowed us to be at our assigned lifeguard positions when the campers came for swim time.

The changing area under the dining hall was known as the Fish Den. It was a chilly, damp, soggy, and dark space with a few benches inside. Lightbulbs hung from sockets in the low-lying ceiling. We turned on the lights by pulling on a string hanging down from each light bulb and turned them off by the same process.

After the campers had their swim time, all the lifeguards had their own private swim time, which was great since we had the whole swim area, diving tower, diving board, and raft all to ourselves. Once we were finished with our swim, we would return to the Fish Den to change back into our regular clothes.

One day, I was the first lifeguard to finish my swim. I headed to the Fish Den to change. All the lights were turned off, causing it to be very dark underneath the dining hall. I was still wet from my swim. My hand was fumbling around the ceiling looking for a friendly string to pull on in order to have light. The next thing I knew I was hit with a large jolt of electricity that literally lifted me off of the dirt floor of the Fish Den and knocked me on my butt! Apparently, someone had removed a dead lightbulb and neglected to replace it. My hand found the empty socket, which, for some unknown reason, was still in the on position, electricity flowing through wires and looking for a new home.

I have heard and read about people having experiences with electricity, live sockets, and live wires. Many times, it is reported that once a person makes contact with the source of the electricity they can't let go. Their muscles seize up and are no longer under their control. I guess it wasn't my time to go. Instead of seizing up, I was thrown for a loop! There is almost no sensible explanation as to why I wasn't electrocuted to death when my wet hand and body were exposed to the electricity coming from that empty socket. Thank you, Lord! I'm still here. If you're keeping score, it's Jesse 2, Death 0. (Realizing, of course, that death will be the last one to score—with no overtime allowed!)

FRIDAY NIGHT DANCES

One of the best things to happen at Camp Rotary were the Friday night dances. They bused girls of varying ages from surrounding cities to attend our camp dances.

We had a DJ who spun the platters and played some good old rock 'n' roll! Then . . . there were the slow dances.

The girls sat in chairs on one side of the dance floor and the boys sat on chairs facing the girls on the other side. When the music started, the boys would walk across the floor (a seemingly endless walk) and then ask a girl to dance. Sometimes if the girl said "no" you might summon up the courage (or stupidity) to continue down the line of chairs and ask another girl to dance. After three rejections, everyone in the dancehall realized that you were either a leper, an untouchable, or suffered from chronic halitosis! You had no choice but to return to your original seat. Actually, *this* walk back across the dance floor, with all eyes glued upon me (so it seemed), was the longest walk of my young life, without a doubt.

As luck would have it, I met my first girlfriend at one of the Friday night dances. I was only twelve years old. Not only was it great to have a girlfriend to write back and forth with during the week but there was the added advantage of not having to hear a "no" during the slow dances and not having to face that brutal walk back across the floor. I also took comfort in the fact that I would be asked to dance during the "ladies' choice" dances. I was in dancehall heaven!

The last dance of every Friday night was the infamous "Flashlight Dance." All the house lights were turned off and camp counselors stood on chairs around the dance floor with flashlights. Their job was to catch some of the dancers smooching during the dance. I would always dance next to one of my favorite counselors and ask him not to turn us in with his flashlight ray. I think I had a spotless record of a Friday night kiss without ever getting caught. We would then walk our girlfriends to the waiting buses looking forward to the next Friday night dance. I learned that success often comes through collaboration with others, in this case, a counselor friend with a flashlight!

A spinoff event from the Friday night dances was "Sadie Hawkins Day." It was held every summer on a special Saturday. The Friday night girls were bused in or driven in by their parents to Camp Rotary. (Why does this sound so much like an exercise in conjugal rights in a prison?) The girls would dress like Daisy Mae and the boys dressed like Li'l Abner. (Lil' Abner was a well-known comic strip in the 1950s.)

Each girl packed a box lunch, which she would eventually share with her Li'l Abner of choice. The girls lined up and faced the boys, who lined up facing them about twenty yards away. A cannon shot was the signal for the girls to approach (or chase) the boy of her choice. Once she tagged him, then he became her Li'l Abner for the day and would end up sharing the box lunch with her. If this seems a little hard to believe, I urge you to Google "Sadie Hawkins Day" to learn more about its history.

While this might sound like a simple deal, it was fraught with some challenges in execution. First, if a boy and a girl had already prearranged to be with each other on that day then the boy had to be certain that another unwanted female did not tag him first. This was a logistical challenge that required quick feet and sudden moves to get closer to your predetermined Daisy Mae and finally feel the safety of her tag.

Second, many boys did not have a prearranged rendezvous with their own special Daisy Mae. In fact, there were many who were terrified by the thought of being tagged by a girl they definitely did not want to spend the rest of the day with, for any number of reasons. It's not a coincidence that many of these boys excelled in track and field as they grew older.

Unfortunately, there was always a small group of Daisy Maes who ended up sharing their box lunches with themselves each year. Such was life in "Dogpatch." I learned the value of planning ahead and having one's "ducks in a row" before executing a plan!

THE GIFTS OF CAMP ROTARY

I spent nine wonderful summers at Camp Rotary; however, at age fifteen I finally realized that it was time to leave this segment of my life behind and to move on with my adolescence and all of the new experiences that the future would hold. That having been said, I will never forget the lessons learned over the years I attended Camp Rotary.

I learned about discipline and organization. As campers, we were subject to a daily routine beginning with the sound of the morning cannon followed by the playing of "Reveille" and ending with the playing of "Taps" at nine o'clock every evening.

Every camper took his turn being the "waiter" for his table, which meant that he had to set the table and serve as the food runner when the pots of food became empty during meals. Then it was back to the line at the kitchen to queue up for second or third portions—as long as the food supply held out.

LEE'S TRAILER PARK

Every cabin's table took its turn at drying the dishes for the three meals a day that were served to the 200-plus campers. Dishes came out of the dishwasher scalding hot, needing to be pushed aside till they were cool enough to dry by hand.

After breakfast, each cabin took part in "Squads." This consisted of each cabin being assigned a certain geographical area of the campus or campgrounds and working together in teams to pick up any trash or litter in those areas.

After Squads, it was time to return to our cabins to make our beds and clean up the cabin and grounds. All shoes and sneakers had to be aligned neatly under the bottom bunks. Every bed needed to be made without showing a wrinkle. The floor needed to be swept clean, and the grounds needed to be spotless from litter. Bathing suits had to be tied neatly to the clothesline provided for that purpose.

During the day, every cabin was subject to a surprise inspection, usually when we were out enjoying sports or other recreational activities, thereby leaving the cabins empty. Every cabin started at fifty points, with deductions made for a variety of violations (messy bunks, dirty floors, shoes not in place, litter on grounds, etc.). They would then announce the scores for each cabin during dinner. At the end of every week, one cabin from each age division (Indians, Pioneers, Seniors) would be announced as the winner and receive "free store" (dessert after dinner from the camp store) as a reward.

Taking part in the swim team, baseball team, softball team, rifle team, and archery team taught me the value of teamwork. While I always tried my utmost to be number one in every sport I played, the real goal was for Camp Rotary to win as a team. Our swim team was undefeated for the six years that I was on it. Our baseball team lost only four games in the six years I was on it. Sharpshooting and archery were a little spotty in terms of our team victories, but we all learned to celebrate our wins and to shake hands with our competitors, win or lose, after every contest.

When I became a junior counselor during my eighth year of camp (at fourteen years old), I learned about the value of becoming a good leader. I worked with the campers in my cabin as a group and with some of them individually. The junior counselors had weekly training sessions where we role-played different scenarios that we might face on a daily basis.

I learned that the real secret to success as a leader was the ability to help others achieve their goals and objectives. By helping individuals to succeed, the whole group succeeds.

Not having a full-time father was difficult at times. When we had Father's Day at Camp Rotary, I was the only camper who did not have a father, brother, or uncle to partner with me in the various events. Tony never took part in any of the events because of his bad leg; though his brace and cane never seemed to slow him down from the other things he wanted to do in his life. Thankfully, my cabin counselors served as surrogates and filled the role of a father for me to avoid being left out and alone. Looking back at those formative years, I realize now that the adversities I faced were blessings in disguise. I can now clearly see and understand the meaning of the adage, "The stronger the winds, the deeper the roots."

While not quite hitting on the next Amway or Microsoft, all of my efforts to think creatively and to learn about the challenges of becoming an effective leader and running several businesses served me well over the course of my future endeavors. I would eventually become successful in corporate management and sales and even establish a career as a professional motivational speaker and corporate strategic planning consultant thanks to lessons learned at Camp Rotary.

CHAPTER SIX — "MOVING ON UP"

OUR THIRD TRAILER

While I now spent my summers at Lee's Trailer Park instead of Camp Rotary, the upside of this change came in the form of a new trailer to live in. Somehow, Tony had worked his usual magic and was able to buy a brand-new Fleetwood trailer for us. It was 45 feet long and 10 feet wide. This experience felt like moving from a rowboat to an ocean liner!

Our new home on wheels had two bedrooms, a complete kitchen, and a spacious living room. We now owned the biggest and newest trailer in the park. We even had a larger lot with ample parking and a small plot of grass in our yard.

One day we were having a barbecue outside of our new digs. Tony set up the charcoal grill next to our new trailer and began pouring a can of lighter fluid over the coals. I made the mistake of telling him that I thought the grill was too close to the trailer and that we might want to move it farther away toward the center of our yard. This is when he made it crystal clear that he was in charge and that I was never to tell him what to do under any circumstances.

His reaction to *my suggestion* was to pour even more of the lighter fluid on the coals and then strike a match to ignite the fire. There was this loud WHOOSH as the flames shot out from the grill and lapped at the side of our new trailer. A large section of our new trailer was now missing paint that had curdled up to form a colorful puddle on the ground next to the grill. I was so mad at Tony that I almost bit a hole in my lip!

We eventually had the manufacturer of our now-slightly used trailer repair the damage and repaint the section that was burnt. Lesson learned! Never tell Tony what to do. He will figure it out on his own. Some people would prefer to learn from their mistakes caused by a closed mind than consider suggestions from others who might have something good to offer in the way of advice.

An offshoot of this lesson occurred one day when Tony was driving from our trailer in Revere to nearby Chelsea to pick up my mom from her place of work at the Chelsea Naval Hospital. I was dutifully sitting in the passenger seat making certain that I did not offer any directions or advice even though Tony seemed a little disoriented with the route he had taken to get to our ultimate destination.

We were in a part of Chelsea where train tracks crossed over the cobblestone road that we had ended up on. Much to my horror, I could clearly see an empty boxcar sitting on the tracks up ahead of us. I held on to my seat and braced myself but did not say a word—as previously warned. At the last second, Tony saw the train car sitting in the middle of the road and slammed on the brakes. This helped to soften the blow when his new Cadillac convertible contacted the boxcar.

Predictably, he looked over at me and began yelling because I did not warn him about the train car in the middle of the road in enough time for him to avoid hitting it. I reminded him that he had told me to "never tell him what to do" and that I was afraid to speak up. It was Tony's turn for a lesson learned! Yes, I was scared on the outside but laughing on the inside. Chalk one up for the good guys.

LEE'S TRAILER PARK

LACONIA, NEW HAMPSHIRE

Besides our new (slightly burnt) trailer, one of the side benefits of staying at Lee's Trailer Park during the summers was that I could occasionally spend a weekend or two with Bobby Kelly at his summer campground at Paugus Bay on Lake Winnipesaukee where the Kellys had a vacation trailer. Bobby's parents also provided him with a speedboat, on which we spent most of our days exploring, swimming, waterskiing, and day camping.

Whenever Bobby's father, Mike, was in the boat, he would place his fingers in his mouth and produce a loud whistling sound that would get Bobby's attention in a big way. Mike had an issue with his voice- box, thus the whistling. When Bobby would turn back to the stern of the boat to look at this father, he would see him waving his hands up and down and mouthing the words "slow down," which both embarrassed and infuriated my blood-brother. Most of the time we were without Mike on board, so it was "damn the torpedoes and full speed ahead!"

I spent some of the best days of my life on Bobby's boat on Lake Winnipesaukee playing, laughing, water skiing, and just having a blast. For some strange reason, whenever it was my turn to ski behind the boat, Bobby liked to play this game called "the whip." He would max out the speed of the boat and then take a sharp turn, thereby forcing me out of the safety of the wake and throwing me into the onset of an inevitable disaster at unbelievable speeds, sometimes up to forty miles per hour! Eventually, my shaky legs would give way and I would tumble over the water like a bowling ball on a cement sidewalk, with no end in sight.

Bobby and his friends would laugh so hard that I couldn't help but join in with them. The laughter made me forget about the pain of hitting the surface of the water at such a high rate of speed. How I never ended up with any broken bones is a miracle that I will never fully understand.

THE GAZEBO

Then there were the girls. Including Bobby and myself, the boys numbered four, all of us around the same age of fifteen or sixteen. As luck would have it, there were also four good-looking girls around our age who lived in or around the Paugus Bay campground in the summer.

One of our favorite pastimes was for the eight of us to gather in the gazebo on the trailer park campgrounds and talk. This is how summer romances began. During one of our "talking sessions," the conversation somehow morphed into a somewhat diabolical plan—a sexy plan!

Not too far from the gazebo was a wooden bathhouse. One half of the bathhouse was a toilet facility for women and the other half was for the men. The structure itself had a pitched roof and a dividing wall inside to separate the men from the women. Oddly enough, the wall did not extend all the way to the roof. It only rose approximately eight feet from the floor, just enough to provide separation and privacy when the facilities were in use by both men and women at the same time.

Now, for the plan. It was pointed out that if the guys went into their side of the bathhouse that the girls could also go into their side of the bathhouse at the same time. It was then concluded that if the girls or the guys stood on the top of the toilets on their respective sides that they could then pull themselves up high enough up the dividing wall to see over to the opposite side.

Here's where it gets good! The plan was for the guys or the girls to pull down their pants or skirts so that those on the other side could step up on the tops of the toilets and enjoy the view. After the initial viewing, then the other side would reciprocate, thereby providing a similar experience. After some strenuous negotiations, we decided that the boys would be the first to remove their pants and provide the girls with their view. (We men are so easy!). Then the girls would be next.

I don't know if you can see where this is headed but here it is: Another life lesson learned! We boys gathered on the men's side of the bathhouse and made our way into the toilet area, like four owls on a branch of a tree. As soon as we removed our pants, we could see the chins of the girls lined up at the top of the separation wall with their eyes gawking down at us. Then came the high-pitched squeals of laughter! Next . . . the girls disappeared from the bathhouse, running away while continuing to laugh uproariously.

For the uninitiated, the lesson here is to never agree to be the first one to take your pants off on a dare. You could lose if you do!

WINTER SKIING IN NEW HAMPSHIRE

The good times in Paugus Bay were not just reserved for the summer months. With the onset of winter came the joy and excitement of snow skiing.

I would spend some winter weekends with Bobby and his parents at their Paugus Bay trailer camp. We would devote every day to skiing at some of the great venues nearby such as Cannon Mountain, Cranmore Mountain, and Gunstock Mountain. Somehow, my mom and Tony would come up with enough money for me to pay my way on the weekends that I had been invited by Bobby to go skiing.

When Bobby and I were in high school, I had a long-distance romance with a girl named Janice. She lived in Philadelphia but visited her aunt (Christine) and her grandmother every summer at Lee's Trailer Park, which was where our romance started at an early age.

J. H. JAMES

One year, Janice and her girlfriend, Jane, decided to spend their Christmas holiday at Lee's Trailer Park. This opportunity sparked the idea of Bobby and me heading to New Hampshire with the girls for a few days of some serious skiing along with some other important activities!

Bobby's mom and dad served as chauffeurs and chaperones during the trip. The girls shared a room at the Christmas Island Motel, which was directly across the road from the Paugus Bay Campgrounds. Bobby and I stayed in the trailer with his parents.

Janice and Jane were novices at skiing, so they spent the first half-day taking beginners' lessons while Bobby and I were skiing nearby so we could keep an eye on them (and their Austrian ski instructors!). By the end of the day, and over the course of the weekend, we were all able to ski the intermediate slopes together.

After a long day of skiing and a hot dinner, we would all meander over to the Christmas Island Motel, where we would dim the lights and engage in some heavy bouts of making out with the girls. So much for chaperones! What a way to spend a winter weekend in New England!

I ended up visiting Janice after she returned home to Philadelphia, but after a time, our communications and contact seemed to drop off. I finally met her again for dinner in Florida in my forties. It was then that I learned that the past is something that cannot easily be resurrected, at least in most cases . . . with this being one of them. Still, it was good to see her again and talk about the great times we had shared together at Lee's Trailer Park in the summers and on the slopes of the ski resorts in New Hampshire that one winter.

OUR NEW HOUSE

By now, I was a junior at Revere High School. Up to this point, I had spent virtually my entire life living either in a Quonset Hut or in trailers on wheels. It was time for another "moving on up" experience!

Much to the surprise and delight of my mom and me, Tony arrived at our trailer and announced that he was buying a house for us in Squantum, Massachusetts, which is next to Quincy in Boston's South Shore—the polar opposite direction from where we were currently living in Revere on the North Shore.

The next day, the three of us drove to Squantum to see our new home: three bedrooms, two baths, a den, and a spacious living room. It also had an enclosed garage. It was unbelievable! I had never been so thrilled in my entire life.

I had a big bedroom all to myself. It was on the second floor overlooking the large yard behind the house. The yard even had a tree in the middle of it. There was a white picket fence and all the curb appeal that you would expect from a home in this upper/middle-class neighborhood in the South Shore of Boston. The house was less than a mile from the Atlantic Ocean.

I was so excited that I couldn't even think straight. All of my focus, thoughts, and efforts were centered on our new house in Squantum. I would attend North Quincy Regional High School, which was very highly rated academically. It was also a huge step up from Revere High School (RHS) and the daily fistfights at the close of school.

RHS was where I learned to maintain a low profile and to stay out of harm's way by keeping my friends close and my enemies closer! I don't remember feeling any greater pride or enthusiasm in my young life than I did when I learned about our new home. This would be a gas!

With little prodding or strategizing, I took it upon myself to announce to my friends and classmates that I would leave RHS and move to Squantum within the next week. I then began checking myself out of RHS, returning my books, and saying my goodbyes.

My mom wasn't happy that I was moving at such a fast pace. However, I have never been one to let the grass grow under my feet. Besides, checking out of RHS quickly would give me more time to help with the move and to settle into our new neighborhood before starting school at North Quincy Regional.

It was a Saturday morning and my mom and I had just completed loading up her car with packed boxes and incidentals to take to our new home. This was our fourth trip to move some of our prized possessions (stuff!) to the new house.

We made the drive through the Sumner Tunnel under Boston Harbor and headed toward the driveway of our new home. Here is where a major problem was about to rear its ugly head.

In the driveway sat a sheriff's car blocking our entrance. Mom parked on the street in front of our house and made her way to the front door where she was greeted by the sheriff himself. She almost dropped the potted plant that she was holding but turned in my direction (as I was now standing beside her) and handed it to me.

The sheriff had some terrible news for us. Evidently, Tony's deal for the house wasn't a clean one. The sheriff mentioned something about bad checks and the word "extortion," which I did not completely understand at the time. What I understood clearly was that the house was not legally ours nor would it ever be ours. Charges were being filed against Tony, and the current owner of the house was threatening legal action against both Tony and my mom.

The word "impounding" hit my ears. They were threatening to keep all of our personal items that we had taken to the house over the course of the past few days. Mom was a wreck. I was a wreck. Tony was nowhere to be seen or heard of.

LEE'S TRAILER PARK

The sheriff eventually allowed us to leave but assured us that this was not the end of the story. The ride back to Lee's Trailer Park was the longest and most desolate one that I could ever remember. Mom was in tears, and I was close to joining her at any second; but, I decided that I had to be strong and help us get through this somehow.

My feelings included anger, resentment, embarrassment, confusion, and a huge sense of loss. My thoughts were now filled with how I was going to re-enroll at Revere High School and what I would tell my friends, classmates, and teachers when I returned. Talk about eating some humble pie! WHEW!

Somehow, someway, I made it through this crisis in my adolescent life. There's that old saying again, "whatever doesn't kill you will make you stronger I felt I was becoming strong enough to join the Olympic weightlifting team! Life moves on . . . and so it did.

J. H. JAMES

CHAPTER SEVEN — "OFF TO MAINE"

TONY'S NEWS

It wasn't long after the infamous "we almost had a house fiasco" that Tony moved his aluminum siding business to Maine, where he opened an office in the city of Saco. Before officially making the move, Mom and I would make the two-hour drive from Revere up to Scarborough on the weekends. The cottage motel that we stayed at was only twenty minutes from Tony's office. Tony and Mom had their cottage, and I had my own as well.

The motel had a swimming pool, which was more than enough to placate me as I loved to swim and could spend the better part of a day in the water. The pool also had a diving board, which added to the fun on these getaway weekends.

I was a fairly good diver and would dive with Ron (one of Tony's salesmen) when he stopped by to visit the cottages and make use of the pool. I actually taught him how to do forward flips and back-dives from the board. Most of his entries into the water were horizontal, which kept us all in stitches (and fortunately he never required any himself)!

One morning, I left my cottage and headed toward the pool. As I looked ahead, I noticed something floating in the middle of the pool.

Eventually, I was close enough to see that it was a small girl lying facedown in the water.

I immediately jumped into the pool and swam over to her. I moved her to the shallow end using a life-saving stroke that I had learned at Camp Rotary. I then lifted her out of the pool and onto solid ground as I yelled for help and asked someone to call 911.

Even though I had been trained in life-saving techniques and CPR, I panicked in terms of what specific steps to take next. I flipped the young girl (seven years old) onto her stomach and put her arms down beside her with her elbows pointing out. I then began pushing down in the middle of her back, followed by pulling her elbows upwards. I repeated this process again and again while waiting for help to arrive.

Finally, the girl began coughing and spitting out water just as the ambulance arrived. The EMTs took over (much to my relief) and continued the resuscitation process in a much more professional way.

The girl survived her near-drowning incident, and I had done my part to save a human life from certain death. Little did I know that in forty-five years, I would again jump into a pool to pull another person from the water and out into safety. This time it would be the woman I love more than anyone or anything in the world, my wife, Ashlee!

THE PERMANENT MOVE

The weekend treks to Maine and back to Boston began taking their toll. It was summer in New England, and I was rapidly approaching the start of my senior year at RHS. My mom and Tony had decided to pick up our home on wheels and move our trailer to a park in South Portland, Maine, during the summer and before the start of school.

LEE'S TRAILER PARK

I would finish my senior year at Scarborough High School (SHS). Scarborough was a small town next to South Portland and was part of the school district that they assigned me to. At least this time I would not have to check out my books and transfer during the school year.

Becoming a student at SHS was truly a culture shock for me. There were fewer than 400 students in the entire school. At RHS, there were almost 500 students in my graduating class alone! There would be only 150 students in our graduating class at SHS!

Also, the transition from a big high school in a fairly large suburban area close to Boston, to a small rural high school in the middle of the boondocks in Southern Maine, was not an easy one to make . . . different lifestyles, values, activities, outlooks, and behaviors entirely. Culture shock!

During the first day of school, the bell rang to signal the changing of classes. I quickly made my way to the men's room and lit up a cigarette after entering the bathroom. All the boys in the bathroom stood motionless, staring at me as though I had just brought a bomb into the school!

While smoking in school was not allowed at RHS, it was a rite of passage. The gray clouds of smoke wafted out into the halls in between classes, but the teachers never invaded the students' private space. Smoking at RHS illegally was a given (just don't get caught). Smoking at SHS was a mortal sin!

I was far from the idyllic student at SHS. Quite to the contrary; I found myself sitting in the principal's office more than in my classrooms. There was a loudspeaker system in the school, and hardly a day went by that you wouldn't hear, "Will Jesse James please report to the principal's office?" echoing from the classrooms and through the hallways. I could also hear the laughter as I made my way down the hallways en route to the principal's office (Mr. Nolan), waving to my friends and fans through the glass windows on the classroom doors.

ESCAPE FROM ALCATRAZ

Somehow, I had worked out my class schedule so that the period before lunch was a free period. These periods were always spent in the library with a teacher/monitor overseeing the students busily working away on their lessons or nodding off to sleep.

When the bell rang to signal the start of the period before lunch, we would all file out into the long hallway (the school was L-shaped, with the long stem of the L creating the hallway) and walk in a straight line with the classrooms on the right side of the hall.

Eventually, we would reach the end of the hall where there was a small alcove with access to a fire door. At that point, we would make a U-turn and continue down the other side of the hall with the classrooms, once again, located on the right side of the hall. Students would drop into their assigned classrooms until the hall was empty and void of any students.

In my particular case, I exited the hallway every time we made the U-turn at the alcove where the fire door was located. I would drop behind the pebble-glassed window at the end of the hallway next to the fire door. When all the other students were safely tucked away in their classrooms, and the coast was clear, I would then exit through the fire door, navigate over a nearby 5-foot fence bordering a field, and then dart across the field, in a crouch, until I hit the main highway where Bette's Place (a local greasy spoon) was my final destination.

Once ensconced at Bette's, I would order up my burgers ahead of the throng of students who would soon join me at the end of their last period before lunch. The added benefit to this maneuver was that I had first dibs on the pinball machine. No need to put a coin in the queue on top of the glass and hope that I might get a game in before heading back to school.

When the students finally made their way to Bette's for the lunch break, I always felt like somewhat of a celebrity. They would throw me a smile and a subliminal high-five as they came through the doorway. I had gamed the system and not one of them seemed to resent it. In fact, they were somewhat in awe of my accomplishment. I felt like the Cool Hand Luke of SHS! No one ever snitched on me . . . not that they had to, as I eventually got busted.

Two of the lessons in life that most of us eventually learn is that nothing is ever perfect and nothing lasts forever. One day, as I dropped into my hiding place near the fire door, a freshman student named Steve crouched down beside me. He wanted in on the scam. I said to him, "What the hell are you doing here, man? You need to get your ass to your next class!"

He looked at me with his freshman puppy-dog eyes and said, "I want you to teach me how this is done." Realizing that we all have a legacy to leave, I let him tag along.

The halls emptied, and we made certain that the coast was clear—usual procedure. We went out the fire door and jumped the fence. When we started running across the field, Steve drifted far out to the left of me instead of staying directly behind me. It was critical when making the run that you kept the end of the hallway in perfect alignment behind you, thereby avoiding detection from classroom windows on the sides of the hallway.

We made it to Bette's and ordered lunch. He thanked me and bought me a soda. I told him that now that he had the secret, he could use it when I was through with school. It was his to keep in future years after I graduated, but as long as I was in school, I would travel to Bette's Place solo. I was such a thoughtful kid.

When lunch break was over, we all headed back to the school and reported to our homerooms before the starting bell for afternoon classes. Once we settled in, the speakers in each room crackled with an important announcement: "Will Jesse James please report to the principal's office?" Uh-oh!

When I arrived at Mr. Nolan's office, I sat in what had become my usual chair in front of his desk. He looked over at me and said, "You and another boy were seen running across the field at the start of the period before lunch." Double uh-oh!

He then said, "A teacher in class clearly identified you, but he couldn't make out who was running with you. Would you care to tell me who it was that was with you? If you do, I will go lightly on your detention time to be served."

Without hesitation, I looked Mr. Nolan squarely in his eyes and said, "I heard footsteps behind me but never looked back because I thought it was you trying to catch me!" He did his best to stifle a smile but couldn't help himself. He knew that asking me to snitch on someone else was an exercise in futility. He sentenced me to two weeks of detention. No more early lunches at Bette's Place. Case closed!

THE RIFLE

Living in Maine was a totally different experience than living in Revere. After school, many of the students would take to the woods with their hunting rifles in search of squirrels, rabbits, or any other small creature that was "in-season."

Sometimes the trips to the woods would be just for target practice to prepare for the "real" hunting seasons—deer and turkey—approaching in the fall. I would often tag along with Eric, one of the boys living in our trailer park, who had a rifle and would let me join in on some target practice occasionally.

I never owned a gun but was an exceptionally good shot thanks to my years spent at Camp Rotary. I had achieved the rank of "marksman" and had a place of honor on the rifle team at that time.

One day, Tony pulled up in our driveway shortly after school let out. He asked my mom and me to take a ride with him. We ended up in some sand pit surrounded by trees. There was an embankment on the side of a large hill approximately twenty to twenty-five yards from where we had parked.

Tony made his way to the back of the car and popped the trunk lid. Inside were several hubcaps and a .22-caliber rifle and boxes of bullets. He instructed me to take three of the hubcaps to the embankment and set them in a horizontal position, side by side, about three feet apart from each other.

I accomplished my mission then returned to the car and watched Tony as he loaded the .22 with bullets. He braced himself on the hood of the car and shot at one hubcap. The pinging sound of lead hitting metal echoed off the hill behind the embankment as the bullets found their mark.

He then reloaded the rifle and handed it to my mom. It was her turn to shoot. While not an expert by any stretch of the imagination, she inflicted some damage to the hubcaps. Not bad for a stay-at-home mom.

Tony took the rifle from my mom, reloaded, and then looked at me and said, "Would you like to try it?" He handed me the rifle and I happily took it from him and positioned myself against the car. I was able to place a grouping of seven bullet holes inside an area the size of a donut in the center of one of the hubcaps. I'm uncertain if Tony was impressed or upset that I had outshot him. He never said a word.

After an awkward pause, I looked at Tony and asked him, "Could I please have the rifle to keep as my own?" I said this realizing that he was not about to take up target shooting as a hobby and realizing he knew that many of the kids my age owned rifles in Maine.

Tony looked over at me and said, "Actually, I was going to give you the rifle if you hadn't asked for it. Since you have asked for it, then I'm going to say no!" I was stunned. I was just a kid and could not understand the logic behind being punished for asking for something that I really wanted. I felt that if I never asked him for it that he would probably never offer it to me. Naturally, Mom never interceded on my behalf. Another lesson learned: Blood is not always thicker than water, especially when your bread is being buttered by someone other than your son. Another case closed!

DAVE DYER

Bobby Kelly was back in Revere and also in his senior year of high school. While we couldn't hang out together as we had for most of our young lives, we would remain friends for many years to come. In fact, little did I know that I would see him again in Revere sooner than I had imagined.

At SHS in Maine, I met a very cool kid by the name of Dave Dyer. His father, "Big Joe," was a pattern designer at the local shoe factory in Scarborough. Dave also had a brother named Jo-Ed, who had recently returned home from the Air Force.

Dave's mom's name was Jean, and she was a stay-at-home mom and a top-notch cribbage player. When she wasn't playing cribbage with Big Joe (when he was at work), I would usually take her on in a few games after school let out. She was a terrific player and very hard to beat. Dave would join in on the competition as well. Jean was the champ!

LEE'S TRAILER PARK

Dave and I became inseparable. We were the Butch Cassidy and the Sundance Kid of SHS. We would walk into the Friday night dances at the school gymnasium, fashionably late, and would usually have the attention of many of the girls there. The odor of Schlitz or Old Milwaukee Beer would linger on our breath. We always attended the dances, basketball games, and other events in a properly oiled condition.

Dave's brother, Jo-Ed, would sometimes buy our beer for us when he was around. If not, we had other ways and means of getting our six-packs for the weekend, including the help of an old hermit who lived a few miles from Dave's house. He would buy our beer, and we would reward him by sharing our bounty with him.

We drank beer solely to have fun and never to cause trouble or to become involved in malicious behavior. No property damage. No fights. Just fun. We were happy drinkers, not the destructive kind. That doesn't mean we always found ourselves in the trouble-free zone. Not all decisions made while under the influence of a six-pack of suds were the best!

One Friday night, Dave and I were at his house having a few cold ones with Joe-Ed while Big Joe and Jean were having dinner at their country club. Dave and I knew two girls who were babysitting at a nearby home that night while the parents were also out on the town. So, we called the house where the girls were babysitting, left Joe-Ed behind, and headed over to meet the girls.

We were down to our last few cans of beer and had a pretty neat buzz on when we knocked on the door of the house. The girls laughed and invited us in along with our last two cans of beer, which we promptly shared with them. We were having a great time except for our depleted beer inventory.

We were hanging out in the kitchen when I opened the refrigerator door. Bingo! There were six bottles of beer inside the fridge. Before we realized it, we had consumed 4 of the beers with the help of the girls. Not sound decision-making for sure.

Dave and I hit the road before the parents returned and caught us red-handed. We hoped that the girls could concoct some story without turning us in. Evidently, I hadn't learned my lesson from the peeking incident in the bathroom at Paugus Bay a few years back!

When the dad noticed his missing beer the next day, the girls told him that Dave Dyer and his friend Jesse dropped by and drank his beer. Not good!

One of the girls had called Dave on Saturday morning and told him that we would probably be in a heap of trouble. The dad planned to call Big Joe to let him know what we had done. We put our heads together and decided that the best approach would be a proactive one rather than a reactive one.

It was still early Saturday morning, and we were with one of our friends by the name of Steve Wikel. Steve was a senior in our class and had a voice that was deeper than the Grand Canyon! Big Joe and Jean were at the country club playing golf, a Saturday/Sunday ritual. Dave's house became the headquarters for our operation.

We rehearsed the plan with Steve, and he was all-in in terms of trying to pull it off. We gave Steve the phone number and remained quiet as church mice when he began to talk. He said, in his deepest voice, "Hello, Mr. Gordon. This is Joe Dyer, Dave's father. Dave has told me that he was at your house last night visiting your daughter and her friend who were babysitting for you."

Keep talking, Steve. "He also told me that he and Jesse got a little carried away and drank some of your beer while they were there. Let me assure you that both Dave and Jesse will be punished severely for what they did. I've already talked to Jesse's parents about this as well."

Now for the coup de grâce! "Besides being punished, I am sending both of the boys over to your house to apologize and to replace the beer they consumed."

Evidently, Mr. Gordon said that it would not be necessary to replace the beer as long as all the parents knew of what happened and would take disciplinary action against Dave and me. But Steve Wikel had the Oscar Awards in his sights. He said, "Mr. Gordon, I insist that the boys replace the beer they took by using their own money and apologize to you in person."

Mr. Gordon finally caved and said, "OK. I will be here for the rest of the morning and then I have some errands to run this afternoon."

Dave's brother, Jo-Ed, bought a six-pack of Budweiser for us, and Dave and I drove it over to the Gordons' house. Mr. Gordon greeted us at the door with a scowl. We sheepishly apologized for our actions and assured him nothing like that would ever happen again.

Actually, I briefly thought that maybe we should have only replaced the four beers we drank instead of six thereby, leaving another two for us, but I quickly dismissed that as another potentially egregious error in judgment on my part. We were lucky to get out of this whole mess unscathed. Thanks, Steve. You were a great "dad" to Dave and a great help to both of us.

Dave and I continued our escapades throughout the school year. One of our favorite things to do was to buy a case of beer on Saturday morning and to head out on a road trip to other cities in Maine such as Farmington, Sebago Lake, or some other cool destination, in search of adventure, fun, and girls—not necessarily in that order. I will always have very fond memories of our weekend adventures.

J. H. JAMES

SHS — OUR CLASS TRIP

They held our senior class trip in New York City during the opening of the World's Fair in 1964. Imagine a busload of country kids from Scarborough, Maine, heading to the Big Apple for five days of fun, frolic, food, and foam (beer). Oh, I almost forgot—and the World's Fair itself.

Naturally, such an event would require us to have chaperones. Our male chaperone was one of our favorite teachers, Mr. Demers, who was in his early thirties. Our female chaperone was his fiancée! This is sometimes what is known as "the fox watching over the chicken coop." It would definitely prove to be an interesting trip.

Our chartered bus took us to the front entrance of the Henry Hudson Hotel on West 58th Street. We'd barely finished unpacking when one of the brightest girls in our class, a National Honor Society member named Nancy, started introducing herself to many of the young bellmen at the hotel. She would not be seeing a lot of the World's Fair during our stay in NYC! Lessons: You never really know someone until you really get to know them. Also, it's true, "You cannot judge a book by its cover!"

Within the first twenty-four hours of our arrival at the Hudson, there were many changes in room assignments. Those who were in a serious dating relationship ended up as roommates, including our chaperones.

Almost immediately adjacent to our hotel was an Irish Pub called McGovern's. This became headquarters for Dave Dyer, me, and some other adventuresome members of our group. While the drinking age in NYC was 18 in 1964, I was only 17 (a few months away from 18) years old at the time. This resulted in my having to use a friend's driver's license since he did not take part in the class trip (Jimmy Mater). While there was not much of a likeness between his driver's

LEE'S TRAILER PARK

license photo and me in living color, our bartenders at McGovern's were very friendly and also quick to approve the ID card.

Little did we know that the bars in NYC stayed open until four a.m. They were required to close for two hours before opening again at six a.m. I think that the bars in Scarborough, Maine (all three of them), closed at midnight in 1964. They definitely did not open at six a.m., except for some of the dive bars at the docks in Portland, Maine. Seems like fishermen are always thirsty.

Anyway, Dave and I came up with the brilliant idea of closing down the bar at McGovern's one night and then venturing out for a famous NYC breakfast before heading off to the World's Fair that day. As I recall, the breakfast consisted of three eggs, bacon, sausage, home fries, toast, and coffee for the sticker-shock price of $1.99. Gotta love the Big Apple.

After working our way through breakfast and the groggy McGovern's-induced haze that filled our heads, we headed out to the World's Fair. Our first adventure/ride was "A Trip to the Future." There were individual chairs with speakers that narrated different parts of the future as we moved through the exhibit on a slow-moving treadmill.

While the exhibits in front of us were backlit, the area where the chairs moved was dark. Dave fell asleep in his chair during his trip forward in time. Fortunately, my chair was ahead of his, which gave me time to jump out and wake him before he traveled through the exhibit again. If it wasn't for my rescue, he may have cycled through the exhibit for the next day or so.

We left the ride and slowly moved toward the huge fountain with a sculpture of the world, which was the centerpiece of the Fair. We sat on the edge of the fountain and splashed cool water on our faces in a failed attempt to revitalize ourselves. It turned out to be a long, hot day moving from one exhibit to another, albeit at a snail's pace. McGovern's was a site for sore eyes when we finally returned to the Henry Hudson. Cold Bloody Marys helped ease the pain of what proved to be an unforgettable hangover. Live and learn (the lessons kept on coming)!

In addition to McGovern's, Dave and I experimented with something called "Thunderbird Wine," which his brother had highly recommended. Jo-Ed swore by the price and the results based on his experience with this evil potion when he was in the Air Force. We learned the old saying, "What's the word? Thunderbird. What's the price? Thirty twice."

Yes, sixty cents a bottle! We bought two to take back to our room. One sip of this whine (intentionally misspelled) would make you feel like the inside of a Zippo lighter. This stuff was the most horrible substance I had ever ingested. Forget AA, just put everyone who wants to quit drinking on a liquid diet of Thunderbird, and they will swear off alcohol within two days. We never finished the first bottle, and the second one went down the sink. Back to McGovern's!

DANNY BROY

Besides Dave Dyer, one of my very close friends lived in the same trailer park as we did in South Portland, Maine. His family consisted of a stepfather, a younger brother, and his mom.

Danny was a year behind me in school, not that he was younger but because they had held him back one year for poor grades. What Danny lacked in intellect and focus on his studies was more than made up for by his good looks and outstanding body. Danny was a weightlifter and a real ladies' man.

Together, Danny and I were unstoppable when it came to finding girls. On one two-week stretch during summer vacation, we had more than fourteen dates between us. Two of those girls were

Roxanne and Dianne, French twins from Montreal on vacation with their mother in Old Orchard Beach. I paired up with Dianne, and Danny went with Roxanne.

One night, I stopped by their cottage at Old Orchard Beach to see Dianne, but she was out shopping with her mother, thereby leaving Roxanne home alone. I really wasn't certain what to do when she invited me into the cottage.

After I entered the living room, Roxanne said that Dianne and her mother "would be out for a while." It wasn't long after that when we both ended up on the couch making out. My poor judgment (a nagging habit at that age) quickly became obvious when the screen door to the cottage opened and Dianne and her mother walked in on us. I had only one year of French in high school but was quickly introduced to another dark side of the language in a heartbeat. *Sacrebleu!*

That was the last that I would ever see of Dianne and Roxanne. Their mom made the best sweet corn on the cob in the world. She is the one who taught me to add a tablespoon or two of sugar to the water when boiling the corn, something I still do to this day.

Danny and I were kept pretty busy back in those days, trying to keep all the date plates spinning at the same time. Challenges worth having!

After Dave and I graduated from SHS, I would end up spending more time with him and less with Danny as he still had another year to go before he was scheduled to graduate in 1965.

J. H. JAMES

CHAPTER EIGHT — "TONY IN MAINE"

TONY'S OFFICE

Tony had opened his office in Saco, Maine, which was approximately twenty-five miles from the trailer park in South Portland where we lived. He enjoyed having his freedom and anonymity, which the distance between work and home allowed him to accomplish nicely. He had a salesman named Ron (my diving buddy) and a gorgeous secretary named Anita.

As was the case when we lived in Revere, Tony's work seemed to require enough travel that he wasn't home all the time. (Praise the Lord!) There's that anonymity thing he liked so much coming into play again.

He also bought a 44-foot Chris Craft cabin cruiser, which was moored at the yacht basin in Saco. He and my mom would occasionally go out on the boat. Tony was not much of a boater, which explains why they had to be rescued by the Coast Guard when they became stranded on a sandbar during one of their excursions.

He had the boat for the two years we lived in Maine, but I never once stepped foot on it. In fact, I never even laid eyes on it, which was OK with me. The less time with Tony the better, as far as I was concerned. Something tells me that there was probably a .22 caliber rifle on board that boat somewhere!

J. H. JAMES

CHICKEN POT PIE

Among a multitude of other things, Tony was a well-known gambler and often sat in on a big poker game, a craps game, or an Italian card game when the opportunity presented itself. On one particular day, he had made a big score and was carrying more than six thousand dollars in cash when he came home very late in the evening. I was already in bed in the arms of Morpheus.

By this time, Mom was getting really annoyed at Tony's extracurricular activities (which she suspected may have included his new secretary, Anita) and his many nights away from home. It's safe to say that Tony was not on her "good boy list." In fact, he was on her other list . . . the one I tried desperately to avoid being on at any point in time.

In the middle of one of my school nights, my mom came into my bedroom and rustled me awake. With my eyes still heavy from sleep, I said to her, "What is it?"

Mom put her index finger over her lips and said, "Shush, he's still asleep."

"OK," I whispered. "What's going on?"

"We are going to rob Tony," Mom replied.

I immediately said, "What is it with this 'we' talk? As in you *and me*?" I asked.

"Yes," she said. "I need your help in deciding where to hide the money! Just wait here a minute. I'll be right back." It's not as though I had other plans that evening other than to wake up in the morning and head off to school. So much for that line of thinking!

Mom left my bedroom and headed for their bedroom, which was only ten feet farther back in our trailer. She took the six grand from Tony's pants pocket and opened some of their bureau drawers while messing up their room to make it look as though someone had come into the trailer during the night and robbed him. Tony was obviously a sound sleeper, which they say is unusual for people with a guilty conscience and a track record of nefarious behavior.

Mom returned to my bedroom with the cash in her hands. "Tony made a big score and came home with this," pointing to the cash. She then waved me into the kitchen. "OK," she said as she looked squarely into my face and asked, "Where should we hide it?"

The sting was on. I was hooked. If you've never been in a situation like this in your life, then that's probably a good thing. No matter where you think of hiding the stolen cash or property, you ultimately conclude that it would be the first place the victim would look, assuming they became suspicious that there was a scam underway from the inside, not the outside.

It was summer, so we thought about hiding it in the heating stove under the burner. No, he would definitely look there! What about in one of the old photo albums tucked away in the top of a closet? No, definitely too obvious. How about under the couch? Definitely a no.

Without uttering another word, I calmly stood up from my chair at the kitchen table and walked to our refrigerator. Mom's eyes were totally fixated on my every move. I opened the refrigerator door and then did the same with the freezer door inside the fridge. This is when I deftly removed a Morton's Chicken Pot Pie from our freezer.

Mom remained speechless, but her eyes were sparkling with joy as I took the pie out of its box and removed the pie crust from the aluminum heating container, and set it aside for the time being. I then scraped out all the inside of the pie, which would eventually be flushed down our toilet. I took the money (four Grover Clevelands and twenty Benjamin Franklins) and lined the pie heating container with the bills before carefully replacing the pie crust back over the container.

Then I placed the container back into its original resting spot inside the box. I used a small piece of doubled-over scotch tape to reseal the box and placed it back into the freezer. Good as new! There it was, safely hidden away, six thousand dollars in "cold cash!"

Mom finally started breathing again. She said to me, "OK, you head to bed and go back to sleep just as if nothing has happened." (As though that would be humanly possible.) "I will slip back into bed with Tony and wait until he wakes up first. We need him to discover the robbery, not us."

It seemed like an eternity as I lay on my back staring at the ceiling while waiting for Tony to awaken. My palms were sweaty, and my breathing was labored. Finally, I heard Tony yelling, "Boobla!"—his nickname for Mom—"Boobla, wake up," as he immediately reached for his pants that were now in a pile on the floor of their bedroom.

Their bedroom drawers had been tossed and the front door to the trailer was open. His instincts were right—the money was missing, and he shouted out, "We've been robbed!"

I pretended to be roused from my sleep by the commotion and said, "What happened? What's going on?"

The three of us met at the kitchen table. Tony was trying to determine who was responsible for the robbery. He eventually said, "Only Ron knew that I had that much cash with me last night. It must have been him that set this up. I know how to handle this. He will regret the day that he tried to cross me."

Uh-oh! A monkey wrench had just been thrown into our machinery. The handwriting was on the wall. If Tony believed that Ron had engineered the robbery, there would be a better-than-average chance that Ron's knees would no longer be in good working order sometime soon. Worse yet, he might get an unexpected ride on Tony's Cabin Cruiser.

I peeked over at Mom, and she returned my glance with a look of acknowledgment and resignation. It was her turn to leave the kitchen table and walk toward the refrigerator. There is no way in the world that I can describe the look on Tony's face as my mom opened the chicken pot pie, removed the crust, and showed him the cash. He was totally speechless.

Fortunately for me, Mom did not throw me under the bus. She took the rap completely on her own and used the occasion to let Tony know that she had done it because she was so upset at his abhorrent behavior. Lesson learned: This is how a smart woman turns a defeat into a victory. Pretty clever.

I slinked away from the table after the money was taken back out of the chicken pot pie box. It was off to school for another average day of obtaining an education—not that I didn't already have one from the life I had lived with Mom and Tony.

TONY'S SECRETARY — ANITA

Tony's new office in Maine included a new drop-dead gorgeous secretary by the name of Anita. I don't know where he found her, but I had a hunch that it wasn't a typical employment agency. The few times I was in his office, I never saw her place her well-painted nails on the keyboard of the typewriter.

I think Anita's main tasks were to answer the telephone, open the mail in the morning, and send out the mail in the afternoon. Obviously, this required the ability to lick postage stamps, which seemed to be one of the few natural talents in her skill set (at least that could be seen on the surface).

Mom always had a sixth sense about things in life. Her instincts were solid.

One day, Mom dropped in on Tony unexpectedly in the middle of the afternoon. When she arrived at his office, neither his car nor Anita's were in their usual parking spots. On a hunch, Mom drove down to the marina where the Cabin Cruiser was moored.

Lo-and-behold! Both Tony's and Anita's cars were parked in the marina. "Don't come a-knocking when this boat's a rocking!" They were caught red-handed, unless, of course, Anita was planning on performing her typing tasks on the boat!

Rather than barge in and attack (which was definitely an option, knowing Mom), she elected to drive back to the trailer and confront Tony when he returned home that evening. I think she wanted to see him sweat before dropping the guillotine.

I had retired to bed with another full day of school waiting for me in the morning. Mom had not mentioned a word to me about the suspected rendezvous between Tony and Anita. As usual, Tony came home late that night.

Once again, I was yanked from the arms of Morpheus when I heard Tony loudly begging, "Please, Boobla, don't shoot! Put the gun down."

I left my bed and looked down the hall toward their room. The door was open, and I could clearly see Tony on his knees with his hands together in prayer as he blurted out again, "Boobla, don't shoot! I didn't do anything wrong."

Tony had once told me that it was best to deny anything and everything that you may have done wrong, even if you get caught in the act. He said to me, "Let's say you are in bed with another woman and your wife walks in on you. What you should do is quietly get dressed and walk out the door as though nothing has happened. From that moment on, you need to firmly and consistently deny any wrongdoing. Eventually, your wife will begin to wonder whether or not she's losing her mind." Oddly enough, it would be many years before I discovered that this was a strategy invoked by many of the so-called leaders of our country.

With no trepidation whatsoever, I moved toward their bedroom and quietly said, "Mom, don't shoot him. It will create a real mess in more ways than one." Maybe it was my presence in the room, or maybe she just thought better of the consequences of shooting Tony. At any rate, she put the gun down on her dresser and began to sob.

I went back to bed to try to get some sleep before rising early for school and another day of more traditional education.

TONY'S HEART ATTACK

Tony was in his early forties when I was in high school in Maine. While he was overweight, he was still strong as an ox. There wasn't anyone that I ever remember beating him in an arm-wrestling contest. Even my Uncle Harry, who spent his life in the Navy and was undefeated when it came to arm wrestling, could not beat Tony. This caused Uncle Harry great consternation as he hated to lose, especially to someone who had a physical weakness such as walking with the aid of a leg brace and a cane.

Strength notwithstanding, Tony's eating habits, lack of exercise, and stress levels were taking their toll on him. Finally, the cork popped, and one day Tony had a heart attack. He somehow drove himself to the hospital in Biddeford, Maine, where he was admitted, diagnosed, and receiving treatment. Beyond anything else, Tony was a determined man.

Naturally, Mom went to visit him while he was in the hospital. On the second day of his soon-to-be short stay, Mom walked into his room only to find another woman standing beside his bed.

Mom asked, "Who are you?"

The woman replied, "My name is Betty. I am Tony's wife. Who are you?"

Mom responded, "I am Trudy, and I am also his wife." Let the weeping and gnashing of teeth begin!

J. H. JAMES

Up to this point, Tony had been with Mom for approximately twelve years. He had told her that he was married before but had long since been divorced. (You may remember my earlier story of when he brought his two children to my birthday party when I turned seven.)

The shocking realization that he, in fact, was still married, and that his other wife was standing in his hospital room was apparently too much for Mom to bear. Not having been in the room at the time, I cannot attest to the expletives that were bouncing off of the walls when the two wives realized what had been going on for the past twelve years. Quite a juggling act on Tony's part. Living two separate lives with two wives without either of them knowing what the truth was—that Tony was a bigamist. No wonder he was stressed!

Mom eventually made a beeline out of the room and the hospital and drove back to the trailer park. Even though it was snowing, she purposely parked a few streets down from our trailer, thereby leaving no evidence of her car. She was fairly certain that Tony would soon be in pursuit.

As if on cue, just after Mom sat down on the couch in our living room, we could see headlights approaching the trailer. Mom jumped up and went into the closet in my bedroom, which was in the middle of the trailer. She said to me, "Don't let him know I'm here. Just say that I haven't come home yet." What was the name of that song? Oh yes, "Stuck in the Middle with You" by Stealers Wheel.

Tony's car pulled into the parking space next to our trailer. He ambled out into the snow with his leg brace on and his cane in hand. He was wearing nothing but his bathrobe—straight from the hospital. As he entered the trailer, I noticed that I had, once again, contracted a case of sweaty palms. This condition was becoming chronic.

"Where is she?" Tony asked.

I said, "I don't know. I thought she went to the hospital to visit you."

LEE'S TRAILER PARK

As strange as it may sound, Tony began searching the living room thoroughly, even sticking his cane under the coach (under which no human being could fit) and then the reclining lounge chair. He was either definitely persistent or definitely losing it.

I sat at the kitchen table, unable to swallow as he made his way through the kitchen and into my bedroom. He immediately poked his cane under my bed and said, "I know she's here. Where is she?"

He then moved toward the sliding door of my closet. As he began opening it, Mom popped out from the closet and into the bedroom. She scared the living hell out of him! Remember, he just left the hospital where he was being treated for a heart attack, and, at this point, I felt one coming on myself.

Mom bolted out of the bedroom and headed for the trailer door. She was gone in a flash. Tony collected himself and began breathing again. Once settled down, he headed out the trailer door and into his car, still clad only in his bathrobe.

By now, the snow had accumulated to a height of four or five inches. Neither snow, nor rain, nor . . . anyway, you get the picture. Tony was determined to find my mom. She did not head for her car, however. Instead, she left on foot, slogging through the snow. Her destination was a small variety store at the entrance to the trailer park, about 150 to 200 yards from our trailer. She had enough lead time on Tony to avoid being seen from his car as he started his search for her.

As though pulled by a magnet, Tony's car drove up to the variety store, where he exited his car and headed inside. The woman who ran the variety store was named Edna and was of Estonian descent. She was a somewhat functioning alcoholic with cloudy hazel eyes and pink-rimmed eyelids. Edna was probably next on the list of potential heart attacks when she saw Tony enter the store in his bathrobe, shouting, "Where is she?" Fortunately, for all concerned,

Mom bumped into some canned goods in the second of the four aisles in the small store. Tony had busted her!

Tony talked her into the car and drove her back to the trailer. We would eventually find out that Tony had followed Mom's tracks in the snow, which led him to Edna and the variety store. Edna was last seen enjoying a healthy pull of whisky from a small brown pint-sized bottle while silently shaking her head from side to side.

It would be much later, after Tony drove back to the hospital to officially check out, that Mom and I would relive the events of the evening in a gale of laughter designed to hide the pain. No one could make this up. You had to be there, and you had to see it to believe it!

Tony's first wife, Betty, headed back to Haverhill, Massachusetts, where she lived with her children. Mom felt she would never see her again . . . or so she thought.

Tony eventually returned home, where he comfortably slipped into his old routine of gambling, philandering, and adultery. He told Mom that he would not see his other wife again and that she was the only woman for him.

I could never understand (and will never understand) what it was that Mom saw in Tony that had kept them together throughout all the trauma they had endured with each other over the years. I wanted nothing more than for Mom to break up with him and for us to go back to Boston.

CHAPTER NINE — ROUSE'S POINT, NEW YORK

THE AMUSEMENT PARK

Dave Dyer and I remained best friends throughout our last year in high school. After graduation, Dave went to work at the shoe factory where his dad had a key management position.

I went to work at Martin's Supermarket in Scarborough. I stocked shelves, collected grocery carts, bagged groceries, and helped in the produce and meat departments from time to time.

Dave and I still hung out together and found time for fun when our working hours would allow it. We were still pretty much inseparable after graduation.

It was the summer of 1964 when Tony approached Mom and me with another one of his plans. He met a big developer (with lots of money) in a place called Rouse's Point in upstate New York, next to the Canadian Border, just south of Montreal.

According to Tony, the developer had built shopping centers but also had an interest in building an RV park with amusement rides on the shores of Lake Champlain where he owned many acres of land. While the developer was way beyond Tony's league, that did not slow Tony down at all.

He pitched the developer on becoming a partner in the project and said that he could get the amusement park put together as his contribution to the project. This was definitely a deal that smelled of "other people's money"!

Tony's idea was to have Dave Dyer and me quit our jobs and move to Rouse's Point to work on the new project. Dave was stitching shoes and I was bagging groceries. What the heck? We were all-in. The next thing Dave and I knew we were in Rouse's Point, New York, sharing a hotel room.

Tony had somehow arranged (through connections with some wiseguys) to commandeer an assortment of amusement rides from somewhere in Vermont. He had obtained a Ferris wheel, merry-go-round, and some small kiddie cars on a rubberized track that would comprise the mini-amusement park to be situated in the middle of the dustbowl that was supposed to resemble a tourist attraction at Lake Champlain.

The Ferris wheel and kiddie cars made it safely to the new park. Unfortunately, the truck pulling the rig with the merry-go-round horses didn't fare so well. Mom and Tony were cramped into the cab of the truck along with the driver. As they made their way through the winding roads of Vermont and headed to Rouse's Point in New York, Tony asked the driver, "How's everything holding up?"

The driver looked into the rearview mirror and uttered the words, "Everything's fine," which were quickly followed by, "Oops, she's gone." The rig had broken away from the truck and all the horses and parts for the merry-go-round had scattered about in the woods of Vermont. Sometimes it's better not to ask in order to avoid jinxing a situation!

The driver pulled over, and he, my mom, and Tony got out on the side of the road. They headed into the woods on foot trying to collect the remnants of what was once all the contents and parts needed for a merry-go-round. The "guys" that Tony went to for "financing" would not be happy about this latest development. He would do his best to keep the accident to himself for as long as possible, as would the driver and my mom.

Anyway, we still had a Ferris wheel and some kiddie cars to work with for the time being. We also had a newly constructed arcade center with pinball machines, Skee-Ball, pool tables, and lots of cool music from a state-of-the-art jukebox. Dave and I ran the arcade and tackled several other chores and duties as needed.

We spent a large part of our day playing pinball for free. We played so much that we reached a point where we never cared if we ever saw another pinball machine as long as we lived! It's funny how quickly things can lose their appeal when they are totally and endlessly provided at no cost. Somehow it takes the fun out of the challenge, whatever it might be. Lesson learned: Better to have some skin in the game. Sacrifice always makes success taste better.

Tony drove back to Revere Beach (which was a famous amusement park back in the day) and scoured the area for a cotton candy concession. This is where he met a nice Jewish man named Sammy. Sammy had his wife and a young child to round out their family. Sammy also had one employee named Ken who helped run the concession stand.

If you haven't figured it out by now, Tony was a master of con! It would not take too long for him to convince Sammy to move his cotton candy, candied apples, grilled burger concession, his family, and Ken from Revere Beach, Massachusetts, to Rouse's Point, New York. They hired a truck and were off to upstate New York within a week.

Everything was up and running (except for the merry-go-round and the unintentionally euthanized wooden horses), and Sammy was turning out his famous cotton candy hand over fist—no extra charge for the stray fly or two that found their way into the colorful streams of fluffy sugar.

J. H. JAMES

CARS AND GIRLS

One of the benefits of working in this godforsaken place was that it came with the periodic use of Tony's white Cadillac convertible. Dave and I had no trouble driving to the center of town in Rouse's Point with the top down and the music turned up. The girls were always attracted to us (or the Caddy), and we made friends with a number of them very quickly.

As 18-year-old kids caught in the middle of the 1960s in Rouse's Point, New York, we were not really focused on what was politically correct. Neither were most grown men at that point in time, sorry to say. If the Caddy attracted the girls, then so be it. Times have changed over the years . . . (Or have they?)

On one Friday evening, Dave and I decided to go to the Friday night dance that was held in downtown Rouse's Point during the summer. (I guess I had become addicted to Friday night dances at an early age). Once again, the grand entrance in the white Caddy did not do us any harm at all. We parked in the street and quickly found a source for some cold beer.

I met a beautiful young girl who was going into her senior year in high school. Her name was Marie. We hit it off immediately.

After sharing some beer and some laughs, I suggested that we take a ride to find a quieter and more private place to talk. She was as eager as I was to make that happen.

I found Dave busily chatting up some other girls and let him know that I would be back for him in a while. He was OK with that and even said, "Don't worry about it. I can always catch a ride back to the park. I'll meet you there later."

So, with Dave's blessing, Marie and I were off to explore some of the farms outside of the city of Rouse's Point. Dusk had settled in and the evening sky was quickly transitioning to dark.

LEE'S TRAILER PARK

I had absolutely no clue where would be a good place for us to park. Suddenly, I saw a dirt road leading to the outskirts of a cornfield. I followed the road and decided that our parking spot could not be seen from the main road—a great place for making out.

I put the top up on the Caddy and turned off the headlights. We were making some serious headway when we were startled by a knock on the driver's side window and a bright ray from a flashlight. I looked up in dismay to see a uniformed officer standing outside the car door.

I powered down my window and tried my best to smile at him. He said, "Do you have any idea where you are?"

To which I honestly replied, "No, sir, actually, I don't." He then asked for my license and registration, which I promptly and politely gave to him.

He shined his flashlight into the car and onto Marie's face. He shined it on my face again. It was then that he said, "You are in Canada! I am with the Canadian Border Patrol." Uh-oh! Not good (again!).

I said, "I'm so sorry, sir. I had absolutely no idea. I am from Maine in the US and was just out for a ride with my friend Marie here. She lives in Rouse's Point."

He advised me that this section of upstate New York was next to the Canadian border and that there were many roads and farms like the one that we were on that would allow access to Canada, although illegally so. Bottom line: We had mistakenly wandered into Canada without the benefit of a passport or visa!

In a somewhat stern manner, the patrolman suggested that I start the car and head back in the direction I had come from. He also said, "I had better not see you again on this side of the border or there will be a price to pay next time."

I dropped Marie off with her friends downtown. Dave was still there, so we hung out for a while as I shared my border incursion experience with him. He was laughing his butt off. WHEW! That was another close one!

THE FAMILY "JULES" AND TONY

After two months in Rouse's Point, it became clear that this would be another one of Tony's projects that was about to bite the dust (literally). There was little in the way of foot traffic at the arcade, the amusement rides, or the food concession stand. There was just Sammy and his family, Ken the laborer, cotton candy, taffy apples, old hotdogs, flies, Dave Dyer . . . and me.

Mom was safely tucked away in our trailer in Maine, as she only visited the amusement park on some weekends. (Very smart woman!) She had taken a leave of absence from her job at Chelsea Naval Hospital, so she could make her own schedule. She could have quit altogether, however, I believe she had the instinctive insight to question how permanent our move to Maine would be over the long haul.

Bill was the big developer who put the RV park together and convinced Tony that there was a huge opportunity in the amusement park and arcade. Plus, they could look at partnering on future shopping center projects in Montreal on the other side of the border.

Jules was the general manager and right-hand man for Bill and his projects. He was a tall, strapping man in his forties. He had the traces of a French accent, which was probably from the influence of the French-speaking Canadians who lived in Montreal and upstate New York.

One day, I was working up in the rafters in the arcade, preparing to hang some crepe paper streamers throughout the building. Tony was directly below me, standing at the counter at the entrance to the arcade. He had a metal toolbox with him on the counter. It contained lots of coins from the arcade—and his gun!

Before I could begin my work in the rafters, in walked Jules. He strutted over to the counter and began talking to Tony. Their voices got louder as the conversation continued. I was invisible in my cranny located above the rafters, So I had a front-row seat over what was happening below.

Eventually, the two men were screaming at each other. Tony said to Jules, "I've never scraped around to earn some nickels, dimes, and quarters in my life! Where are the people? Where is the business you promised?"

Jules replied, "Where is the advance rent that you promised to pay? Where is the merry-go-round and the other rides?"

Tony lifted the toolbox from the counter and banged it back down while opening the lid. He reached inside and grabbed something. I thought that it might be his gun and hoped that an errant shot would not hit me. Instead, Tony pulled out a handful of coins and threw them on the floor in front of Jules. He said, "I'm done with this bullshit. We're out of here!"

Jules said, "Fine with me. The sooner, the better."

I was focusing on not peeing my pants or falling off of the rafters above the mayhem below. At least I wasn't shot, which was a big plus in my mind.

That confrontation marked the end of our upstate New York adventure in Rouse's Point. We packed up everything we had and were out of town in two days.

Sammy, his family, Ken, and the cotton candy concession (without the flies) hightailed it out of town as well. The kiddie rides and arcade stood as a stark memorial to Tony's doomed amusement park.

J. H. JAMES

It was back to Maine for Dave Dyer and me. He would return to the shoe factory, and I would return to Martin's Discount Groceries, at least for the time being. Lesson learned: "All that glitters is not gold!"

CHAPTER TEN — BACK TO BOSTON

REENTRY — SOUTH PORTLAND

Tony jumped back into his aluminum siding business. Dave and I were both working full-time jobs. Mom was at home. "All was quiet on the Western Front," at least for a short while.

Tony put a quick end to the calm when he met an elderly lady by the name of Mrs. Anderson (not her real name) during one of his aluminum siding appointments (also referred to as "sits"). She was a widow and had a lot of money in the bank. Tony quickly concluded that she would be a better investor in his company than an aluminum siding customer.

I'm uncertain what the details were behind Tony's arrest. However, the State Police picked him up and took him to the Alfred County Jail in Maine where he was eventually supposed to stand trial. The newspaper article that reported his arrest, and pending charges of fraud and extortion, referred to him as "Anthony, alias 'Jesse James,' Paciulli!" How my name became involved in this saga was a mystery to me and a huge sore spot with my mom.

Mom paid the bail that was set for Tony, and they released him from jail. My head was spinning (as usual). Who could keep track of Tony and his escapades?

In his accustomed Teflon-Don manner, Tony eventually had all charges dropped and returned to business as usual, with barely a blip on his social radar screen. Rumors had it that Tony reached out to Mrs. Anderson and convinced her of his honest intentions with his usual gifts of gab and charm. He returned most of the money that had somehow found its way into his bank account.

Speaking of blips on the screen, Mom eventually found out that Anita had resurfaced and had, once again, become a part of Tony's extracurricular activities.

ENOUGH IS ENOUGH

Mom had finally had it. She was on tilt!

She decided to leave Tony and take our humble abode on wheels back to Revere and Lee's Trailer Park. This was undoubtedly one of the happiest and proudest days of my young life. Mom had finally summoned the courage, determination, and common sense necessary to make the break with Tony. I was euphoric.

Mom made the arrangements with Lee's Trailer Park for a nice corner lot when we returned. She also hired a trucker to drive our trailer back to Revere. We spent a few days before our getaway "battening down the hatches" in the trailer to make certain that everything would be secure during the trip back to Lee's. I said my goodbyes to my close friend Dave Dyer and some other friends as well.

During the weeks prior to our heading back to Revere, Tony made several visits to meet with Mom in an attempt to talk her out of leaving. Thank God she was resolute and stuck to her guns.

The plan was for me to find a job and enter a college night-school program once we were back in the Boston area. I was pretty excited about what the future would hold for us. Mom would go back to work for the government as a purchasing agent at the Bureau of Labor Statistics in Cambridge, Massachusetts.

When "D-day" finally arrived, the trucker pulled up and hooked up our trailer to his rig. He would leave first, and then we would follow sometime afterward, meeting him at the trailer park on the other end. Off the driver went. We were on our way to a new chapter in our lives.

When it was our turn to embark on our journey, we jumped into Mom's car and headed due south via the Maine Turnpike. Near the end of the turnpike, we were shocked to see our trailer pulled over to the side of the highway. Behind the trailer was a white Cadillac convertible. Tony was sitting in the driver's seat and the truck driver was in the passenger seat. They were eating fresh fruit that Tony had bought on his way to chase down the truck. He had hijacked our home!

When we pulled over behind the Cadillac, Mom jumped out of her car and headed straight for Tony. A huge argument ensued.

Tony was trying to tell the truck driver to turn around and bring the trailer back to Maine. Mom was having no part of that plan whatsoever. She reminded the driver that he was employed by her and that he legally had to bring our trailer to the agreed-upon destination shown in the contract. The driver eventually climbed back into his rig, started the engine, and headed down the turnpike towards Route 1 to Revere.

Tony drove away. However, I was convinced that this would not be the last we would see of him. Unfortunately, I would be proven right.

SETTLING IN

Our trailer ultimately made it to its destination: Our corner lot on 3rd Street at Lee's Trailer Park. "Home again, home again, jiggety jig."

J. H. JAMES

As predicted, Tony's persistence and determination, accompanied by relentless choruses of "I love you, Boobla" finally carried the day for him. We were back in Revere, and Tony was back in our lives. Damn it!

Good news though! Bobby Kelly was still living in the trailer park. We eased right back into our lifelong friendship without skipping a beat. We became beer buddies and avid Boston sports fans—the Red Sox, Bruins, Celtics, and Patriots. Reconnecting with Bobby was a huge plus for me.

Unfortunately, some sad news interrupted my settling-in process. It had to do with my good friend Danny Broy back in Maine. After graduating from SHS, Danny decided to work on a scallop trawler by the name of *Snoopy*. The boat was owned and captained by Edward Doody, whose son, Ron, was a good friend of ours. We had all hung out together from time to time.

Anyway, it was Danny's first and last voyage on the *Snoopy* on July 23, 1965. The boat was out at sea and had just finished bringing in its port nets with a healthy catch of scallops. The crew then focused on bringing in the starboard nets. As the nets approached the starboard side of the boat, it was clear that they had caught something more than scallops.

As they attempted to raise the nets from the sea, they discovered that an old torpedo was tangled in the netting. Captain Doody did everything he could think of to try to free the torpedo from the nets. Unfortunately, he could not raise the nets and then swing them onto the boat as the torpedo was too heavy for the wench on the boat to handle.

After fifteen minutes of trying to separate the torpedo from the nets, the wench gave way and the torpedo hit the side of the boat, creating a huge explosion. There were twelve crewmen on the *Snoopy* that day, eight of whom died plus four survivors who were seriously injured.

Unfortunately, my good friend Danny Broy was one of the crewmembers who did not make it. Ironically, Ron Doody, the captain's son, had fallen ill and could not make the trip. Fate can be fickle and difficult to understand at times.

When I heard the news about the accident and Danny's death, I was completely devastated. They announced that there would be a memorial service the coming weekend for Danny. My mom and I made the drive back to South Portland, Maine, where we attended the church service in which prayers were offered and condolences were made for Danny's passing. Near the end of the service, everyone stood up, walked down the center aisle of the church, and headed toward the altar.

As I approached the altar, I was totally shocked and stunned! Lying in a coffin was my close friend Danny. I had incorrectly assumed that they had not found his remains because of the magnitude of the explosion at sea. In fact, the early reports were that only the four survivors had been found and that the other eight crew members remained missing. When I looked down at Danny, I became completely overwhelmed with a flood of emotions and a stream of tears. He was far too young to have left this good earth of ours. I still miss you, Danny.

HI-HO, HI-HO, IT'S OFF TO WORK I GO

I found a job at Employers Commercial Union insurance company at 110 Milk Street in the financial district of Boston. The job came through an employment agency. I started in the mailroom at a salary of $51.00 per week. They paid us every two weeks, and I netted $81.00 after taxes. Out of that money, I had to pay the employment agency's fee over three months and $10.00

per week for room and board to Mom. Then I had to set aside money for transportation on the subway and for my lunches as well. Obviously, I did not have much in the way of "fun money" left over when all was said and done.

I enrolled at Northeastern University's night-school program which, thankfully, Employers Commercial Union paid for as long as I maintained passing grades, which I made certain that I did.

A great gift from my mom was her dedicated work ethic, which she passed on to me either genetically or through example (or a bit of both). From the first day in the mailroom at the insurance company, my goal was to get promoted to another department as soon as humanly possible.

One of the primary duties of a mail-boy was to act as a courier between some of Boston's major banks and financial institutions. I would report to the cashier's department to receive the transmittals of drafts, checks, and other important documents that needed to be delivered by hand in the early afternoon.

The courier route typically involved five or six separate stops in various sections of Boston, where I would drop off documents at certain banks or financial institutions. A combination of shoe leather and trolley rides were key elements needed to perform the tasks at hand.

When I was being trained by one of the other mail-boys, he explained that the entire route should encompass two and a half to three hours, nothing less. This included stops for a milkshake or time to chat with some of the girls at the various banks. There was definite peer pressure not to excel and to not attempt to complete the document deliveries quickly.

My thinking was completely opposite of what was being told to me during my training by my fellow mail-boys. I felt that if I could work hard and show management that I had the ability to complete the mission quickly and accurately that it would help me obtain a promotion into the accounting department, which I desperately wanted, sooner rather than later.

One day, I was able to complete all of my deliveries and return to the cashier's department in less than fifty minutes! Instead of hearing, "That's great! A job well done," my work was being questioned by the head cashier. The feeling was that the only way I could have completed the route so quickly was if I had dumped some of the documents in the trash or a sewer drain instead of delivering them. I sat next to his desk as he called every bank to verify whether I had made the deliveries. I was careful not to smirk as each call ended with a confirmation that they received the documents as expected.

This proactive work strategy did not inure me to the favor of my fellow mail-boys. In fact, I felt like if I didn't get out of that department quickly that some unexpected misfortune may come my way sometime soon.

Rather than cave in, I continued my strategy of doing every assignment that I was given faster and better than any of my "competition" in the mailroom. In less than three months' time, they promoted me up to the accounting department. I had achieved my goal.

Hard work, extra effort, and extra hours (at my own cost) paid off once again. They chose me to be the administrative manager of a staff of six in the newly formed Employers Group Mutual Fund. I also continued my studies at Northeastern. Lesson learned: Don't let others stop you from being the very best that you can be.

MY BLOOD-BROTHER BOBBY JOINS THE FUN

While I was working at Employer's Commercial Union, Bobby Kelly was working in an auto parts retail store managing inventory, stocking shelves, and helping with sales. I knew that he wasn't that happy with his job and wasn't making that much money there either.

I asked Bobby if he would like to work for Employer's Group Insurance Company. I explained to him that I had good friends in the data processing department and could more than likely get him an interview there. Bobby gave me the green light, and I set up the interview for him. He passed with flying colors and began working in the data processing department a few weeks following his interview.

While we worked in separate departments, we were always having lunch together and hanging out after work. Sometimes we would work overtime and have dinner at Luigi's where we knew the waitress named Trudy (the same one from the trailer park), who would wait on us and push a beer or two our way. The drinking age in Boston was twenty-one, at the time, and we were still only eighteen.

There were a lot of neat-looking girls working at Employer's Group. There were also great parties at Christmastime and near the Fourth of July in the summer. Bobby and I had a blast working there.

THE COMPANY PICNIC PARTY

One summer, the company's annual Fourth of July party was held at the New Ocean House Hotel in Swampscott, Massachusetts. It had function rooms, two huge pools, tennis courts, basketball courts, and a softball diamond.

Bobby was able to take his dad's new Chevrolet Malibu, and I had my 1957 Chevrolet Bel Air. We decided to take separate cars just in case one of us had to take a different route home with an unexpected passenger after the party. It never hurts to plan ahead.

Bobby followed me to the hotel, and we parked alongside each other since that is where the coolers with vodka and orange juice for our screwdrivers would be kept. After day-long activities including softball, swimming, a bellyflop off of the high-diving board by yours truly, a barbeque dinner, and rock 'n' roll afterward, it was time to head home.

The party was over, but the evening was just beginning for me, as I would drive someone named Sherry home from the party. She lived in Quincy on the South Shore of Boston.

Bobby and I met back at the parking lot where our cars were parked before heading out. Suddenly, Bobby was in a panic. He could not find the keys to the Malibu. Bobby, Sherry, and I spent the better part of an hour tracing our steps back through the day to see where his keys may have ended up. Lots of beer and screwdrivers had been consumed, so we all had somewhat of a buzz on. No keys in sight. Bobby said that his parents would kill him if he had lost the keys. Besides, he obviously couldn't drive the car home. Not cool!

We finally went back to where our cars were parked. Suddenly, Bobby said, "I found the keys!" There they were . . . hanging out of the keyhole in the trunk where they had been all day long. Fortunately, no one stole the Malibu. We just wrote it off as too many screwdrivers! Now stone-cold sober, Bobby headed home and I headed to Quincy on the South Shore with Sherry as my passenger.

HALLOWEEN PARTY

Employer's Commercial Union did not pay the best salaries in the world. However, they were definitely a conduit to some great parties and great times. One of the girls working there was having a Halloween party, and she invited Bobby and me to attend. It was a costume party with a prize for the best costume.

I came up with the brilliant idea that Bobby and I should go to the party as a horse. That decision would require that one of us would be in the horse's head section of the costume and the other would be in the "horse's ass" section of the costume. To avoid conflict, we agreed to flip a coin to see who would be in the front and who would be in the back. As luck would have it, I won the coin toss. As I remember, I had called "heads" during the flip, which was somewhat ironic as that is exactly where I ended up in the costume! Sorry, Bobby . . . once a horse's ass always a horse's ass!

We partied hard and eventually headed home. I was driving my 1957 Chevy, and Bobby was a passenger. No separate cars this time. I believe that the Malibu was no longer available for party excursions after the company picnic debacle.

My Chevy was a work of art. It was black and silver with eight cylinders and a lot of get-up and go. The only issue with the car was that it had an ailing transmission and some engine issues that would create smoke from time to time and cause it to stall out while idling. Anyway, we somehow made it safely home and I dropped Bobby off at his trailer.

The next thing I remember was waking up on the floor in the front seat of my car, uncertain how I had ended up there. I opened my eyes and looked up at the front seat only to see a horse's head looking directly into my eyes. Scared the hell out of me!

Apparently, the smoke in the car had built up and caused me to drift off. It was October in Boston, so the heater was on and the windows were closed. Fortunately for me, the car stalled out shortly after I had stalled out. This probably prevented me from dying of carbon monoxide poisoning. My third close call with death. It still wasn't my time to go. No more "horsing" around like this in the future!

Lots of great times in Boston during our younger days. Thanks, Bobby, for being such a great friend and a great blood-brother.

LEE'S TRAILER PARK

THE BLACKOUT OF 1965

In the summer of 1965, Bobby and I were in the cafeteria at Northeastern University having a bite to eat before our night classes began. He had signed up for classes there along with me. Anyway, I had my tray up on the rail where all the food was available for selection. As I moved toward the cashier (I was next in line to pay), all the lights suddenly went out everywhere, including the cafeteria, the school, and the entire City of Boston. Everything was immediately cast into pitch-darkness. We literally could not see our hands in front of our faces. Bobby was in line in front of me and had already secured a table for us somewhere in the dining room.

Thinking on my feet, I somehow pulled my tray off of the rail and miraculously stumbled my way around the cashier's station and into the dining room where I found Bobby waving his cigarette lighter like a small lighthouse somewhere off in a distant sea. I became the beneficiary of a free dinner courtesy of this unexpected blackout. Bobby had, unluckily for him, already paid for his eats before the lights went out. We sat in the dark and finished our dinners then worked our way out into the streets of Boston.

By this time, there were people with flashlights and transistor radios meandering through the human traffic jam and trying to gain information regarding the blackout. Were we being attacked?

We made our way down into the subway where the trains and trolley cars were still running on backup power from generators. We headed back to Employers Group, but they had completely shut the building down, having had no power whatsoever either. Fortunately, the bar at nearby Luigi's Restaurant had candles and was serving drinks. We settled in and listened intently to the radio reports with the other patrons at the bar.

Apparently, we were experiencing a massive blackout that consumed the entire northeast quadrant of the United States, as far west as Detroit and as far east as Boston, north to Canada, and south to DC. It started when a small electronic circuit breaker (the size of a silver dollar) at the Niagara Falls Substation failed, thereby creating a domino effect that caused other breakers and, ultimately, power substations to fail. It was definitely a scary experience and one that I will never forget.

Bobby and I eventually made our way back to the subway and headed home. The lights came back on that evening. All's well that ends well!

Sometime after the blackout event, I left the Employers Group to become an external systems analyst for Prudential Insurance Company. That position quickly led to my becoming a supervisor of more than forty-two people in the dividend disbursement division. I was only nineteen years old and was still attending classes at Northeastern in the evenings.

As they say, "The rest is history." Wherever I worked, including commercial insurance sales later on in my career, I was quickly promoted upward in administrative environments and became the number-one salesperson in every company I held a sales position with. I would become a successful entrepreneur and a professional motivational speaker with corporate clients from all parts of the country and the world, thereby giving me the opportunity to transition to my role as a strategic planning consultant for corporations of all different types and sizes. Thanks, Mom! Lesson learned: Caterpillars can become butterflies, as long as they don't give up their journey and embrace their destiny.

CHAPTER ELEVEN — TONY STRIKES AGAIN

TONY'S BUSINESS

Unfortunately, Tony was still in the picture, and he wasn't fairing as well as me. His aluminum siding business hit the skids—too many irons in too many fires. He was practically broke.

I sold him my 1957 Chevy for four hundred dollars, threw in nine quarts of transmission fluid to boot (for that leaky transmission issue), and (reluctantly)told him to make sure that he cracked the windows when driving.

I ended up buying a new car. As always, Tony eventually climbed out of the rut he was in and moved over to the positive side of the ledger. A win/win for all concerned.

Tony slid back into his flamboyant lifestyle with late hours, days on the road, and his usual extracurricular activities. On one occasion he was gone for more than a week. How could this guy keep up this pace?

THE CASINO ROYALE

Tony's new hunting grounds (business location) became Hartford, Connecticut. We still lived in our trailer on 3rd Street at Lees Trailer Park. As I previously mentioned, he preferred to spend as much time on the road and away from home as humanly possible.

J. H. JAMES

One night, he came home and told us about his new business venture. He was opening a Chinese restaurant in Hartford. He would name it the Casino Royale! Are you with me here? A Chinese restaurant . . . the Casino Royale! Is it my imagination, or was there a bit of a marketing/branding disconnect going on with Tony?

Where he found all the Chinese cooks is beyond comprehension, but he did. Maybe Sammy of cotton candy fame had some connections in Chinatown!

In addition to the restaurant, there was a large oval bar with approximately twenty seats. There was also a small stage and a dance floor—you know, your typical Chinese restaurant. (Not!) In the center of the inside of the bar was a pyramid of shelves stocked with a large assortment of liquor bottles, the most expensive brands placed on the smallest top shelves.

Oh, I almost forgot! There was also a female singer named Sandy who was, of course, a knockout. (Maybe she was related to Anita from Maine?) Mom and I got to meet her in person soon after the restaurant was open for business. We drove to Harford from Revere to be a part of the festivities.

When we walked into the bar section of the restaurant, Tony was sitting at a high top with Sandy. I was only eighteen years old at the time, but I had developed very good instincts based on a long track record with Mom and Tony. I could tell immediately that something was going on between Tony and the singer. Naturally, Mom could also tell right away that there was a lot more there than met the eye—a lot more than singing songs.

Tony waved us over to their table and introduced us to Sandy. We pulled over two more stools, ordered some drinks, and took part in the icy conversation. After two or three rounds, Mom had had enough of dealing with the situation and asked me to drive her home.

We left sort of abruptly and with no real pleasantries exchanged with Sandy or Tony.

We got in the car, and I started to head back to Revere. When we were less than a mile from the restaurant, Mom said, "Turn around."

I said, "What?"

She responded, "You heard me. Turn around. We're going back to the restaurant." Uh-oh!

I did as I was told, which is usually a good idea when you are riding in a car with a potential terrorist!

When we got to the Casino Royale, Mom quickly exited the car with me following closely behind. She walked into the restaurant and made a beeline for the bar.

The next thing I knew, Mom was behind the bar, screaming expletives at both Tony and Sandy. She then extended both of her hands toward the middle level of the glittering pyramid of bottles in the center of the bar. In one fell swoop, she made it almost 360 degrees around the entire bar knocking bottles to the floor where they exploded into countless shards of glass. She dropped her hands down a shelf level and repeated the process. By this time, some of the hired help (not including Sandy) had made their way behind the bar and were trying to restrain my mom.

I politely suggested to her that it might be a good time to leave prior to the police arriving. She reluctantly agreed and we headed for the front door. Still, Mom could not leave without unleashing a new stream of expletives and a series of hand gestures that did not require the use of all of her fingers.

Finally! We were out of there and headed home.

If you think that this was the end of the relationship between Tony and my mom, you would be as mistaken, just as I was at the time.

This dysfunctional relationship had a life of its own. Lesson learned: Love, like life, is truly a mystery.

THE RAID ON HAVERHILL

Some time had passed since the infamous incident at the Casino Royale. As usual, Tony and Mom had somehow gotten back together. As Yogi Berra would say, "Déjà vu all over again!"

One night, Mom and I were sitting in the trailer watching TV when suddenly she looked at me and said, "I need you to drive me to Haverhill." Haverhill, Massachusetts, is a town located approximately thirty miles north of Revere.

I should point out here that Mom was a woman of uncanny instincts. When she had a premonition about someone or something, it turned out to be right on target ninety-five percent of the time. In this instance, her emotional divining rod was red-hot with vibrations. I should also point out that, while never having been there before, Mom knew that Tony's first wife (Betty) and her children lived somewhere in Haverhill.

Off we went on our trek to Haverhill. "Driving Miss Daisy" . . . here we go again! I hoped that this escapade would lead to a much better result than when I drove Mom to the Casino Royale in Hartford some months earlier. My own instincts once again told me that this would not be the case.

When we arrived at Haverhill, Mom asked me to drive around the residential areas of the city. She was looking for the house where Tony's wife was living and had absolutely no clue as to exactly where it would be.

Suddenly, Mom said, "Slow down. There he is!" She had spotted Tony's Cadillac parked in the driveway of an average two-story home on the outskirts of the center of the city. Her divining rod was beginning to smoke! She told me to park on the side of the street and that she would be back soon.

Mom hopped out of the car, walked up to the front door of the house, and rang the doorbell. Although it was nighttime, I could clearly see a woman answering the door and beginning an animated discussion with my Mom. I would later learn that the woman was Betty, Tony's first wife. They had met before, a few years earlier, at the hospital in Biddeford, Maine, when Tony had his heart attack.

Mom then entered the house while I sat in the car wondering what in the world would happen next. It was only a matter of ten minutes or less before Mom exited the house and headed toward the car where I was patiently waiting for her return.

She got into the car and said, "OK, let's go home."

I said, "What happened in there?"

Mom then told me the story. When she walked into the house, she saw Tony sitting on a recliner in the living room. He turned ashen when she stepped through the doorway. Mom thought that he might be headed for another heart attack!

There were four children in the house, not just the two, he had told us about years ago when he married Mom (the two who had attended my seventh birthday party). What a shock to find out that not only was Tony living with both wives but that he also was procreating more children with his first wife at the same time.

Mom had become pregnant through Tony at one point in their relationship. However, she developed peritonitis of the pelvis and lost the baby. She could not have any children in the future. (While I can't speak to her feelings on that, I secretly thought, "Thank God!")

According to Mom, there was also a large brown-and-white dog (Mom had an innate and irreversible fear of dogs) which I suspected was the fully grown version of the puppy that had entered my life, ever so briefly, approximately eight years earlier. Tony had found a home for him after all. Maybe that was his game plan all along.

Mom said that the conversation inside the house was brief, loud, and filled with a string of expletives. At least that was her version of the story at the time. Bottom line: Tony was still living two lives. All of this after he had promised Mom that he would never see his first wife again after he had his heart attack back in Maine.

When you think about it, this was an unbelievable accomplishment, especially when you consider the additional time that he devoted to chasing other women, gambling, and still trying to run his business as well.

Tony never divorced his first wife. Mom never divorced Tony (though, legally, they weren't married). When he married Mom, he officially became a full-time lifelong, bigamist! It was now clear why Tony would sometimes be gone for a week or more at a time. He would be on vacation with his first wife. And there would be times when he would be away for a week or more with Mom while Betty would be the recipient of some cock-and-bull story.

If you now think this was the straw that broke the camel's back and that Mom and Tony were now finished for good . . . you would be incorrect in that assumption. As usual, Tony reappeared at the trailer in a few days' time with his emotional hat in hand and promises of complete fidelity to Mom. She fell for it again, much to my dismay. Anyway, to paraphrase the old saying, "It was what it was!"

CHAPTER TWELVE — REVERE STREET

GEORGE FABBIANO

Bobby Kelly and I began hanging out at a pool hall on Revere Street. The street was over a mile long and connected the American Legion Highway, on one end of the street, to Route 1 and Revere Beach, on the other end.

Somewhere around the middle of Revere Street was George's Billiards. The owner was a dyed-in-the-wool, full-fledged Revere Italian—black leather jacket and shades included. The shades were appropriate, as the owner, George Fabbiano, was somewhat of a shady character.

We played "Kelly Pool" (no connection to Bobby Kelly) for money. In addition to the six pool tables, there was also a card room in the back of the pool hall where we played $1 and $2 five-card-draw for hours at a time. George Fabbiano and his sidekick, Carl, would also join in on the games. For some reason, they seemed to win a lot more often than the rest of us. George also took a five-percent rake for the house from every pot. Overall, I would win more than I lost and loved playing the game of poker.

There was a bigger poker game at night just a few blocks from George's place. The stakes were higher, and the players were better.

I never really had much money left over from my bi-weekly paycheck after paying Mom board, putting aside lunch money, subway fares, gas in the car, etc. Poker was a way of my trying to make a score between paychecks, but, as you might imagine, no one wins all the time. When I did it was great to have the extra money. When I didn't, I would have to borrow money until my next paycheck.

One night, I was sitting in the bigger game playing $2 and $4 five-card-draw. It was getting late into the evening. Suddenly, the back door to the card room opened. In walked none other than—yup—Tony. Mom had sent him out to find me knowing that I was probably locked into a poker game somewhere. I don't know how he found me, but he did. I guess he had a way of getting information from some of the local wiseguys.

Tony let me know that it was time for me to go. I had just been dealt cards with trip tens but would not end up playing the hand. When we got back to the trailer Tony made it abundantly clear that my poker playing days were over, at least on Revere Street and at least for the time being. Out of fear of bodily harm, I retired from poker for a while.

THE SOCCORSO CLUB

George Fabbiano had a cousin by the name of Tony De Marco who lived on Revere Street. Tony was a Revere fireman and also president of the Maria del Soccorso Society, a private club in the middle of the bookie district on Revere Street. The club had a bocce court, bowling machine, a pinball machine, and the obligatory bar!

One day, after a spirited afternoon of poker, George and Carl (George's friend) invited Bobby and me to join them at the Soccorso Club for a few beers. We were under the drinking age at the time, but apparently what happened in the Soccorso Club stayed in the Soccorso Club. After walking in and being introduced to Tony De Marco and the other paisanos, Bobby and I were "good to go" in terms of going in there on our own in the future, which we did with some regularity.

After Bobby joined the Navy in order to beat the draft, I became a fixture at the Soccorso Club and had many great times there over the years. I learned to cook Italian. (A little-known fact is that the men are much better cooks than the women in an Italian family. Same with the French). Every Super Bowl Sunday, all the men would meet at the club and have a feast of Italian food before, during, and after the game.

One year, we had a live pig brought into the club. One of the regulars, Jackie D, took the pig down into the cellar where he expertly cut its throat before barbequing it over a pit of coals out on the bocce court. Something told me this wasn't the first throat that Jackie D had cut, nor would it likely be the last!

I learned to play bocce and several types of Italian card games, each of which was followed by a round of "boss and underboss," a drinking game in which the winners doled out drinks to their friends, but not to the losers or their personal "drys." I became Italian by osmosis and was admitted as the first non-full-blooded Italian member of the club. They even elected me to the position of secretary of the Maria del Soccorso Society.

Many of the local Italian in-crowd frequented the club. State and local politicians could be seen entering and leaving the club on any given day, including Mayor George Colella, who served ten consecutive terms as mayor of Revere.

I became close friends with the mayor and would go to the Saturday Revere High football games with him and his entourage during the football season. We would usually be invited back to the mayor's house after the games, where he had a large, fully stocked bar built in the basement. There was always plenty of food to enjoy as well.

Another frequent visitor to the club was Joseph J. C. DiCarlo. He was my former seventh-grade schoolteacher who left his teaching career to run for a Massachusetts State Senate Seat. He was handsome, intelligent, and extremely articulate. I served on his campaign committee and headed up the volunteer youth movement to help get out the votes for him during the election. He ultimately defeated a longtime fixture in Massachusetts politics, a man by the name of Harry Della Russo (a connected guy!). It was a stunning victory.

Equally stunning was the news that Joseph J. C. DiCarlo would be expelled from the Senate in 1977 after being convicted of extortion. He was the first Massachusetts State Senator to ever be expelled. I was totally devastated, as I had looked up to him as a mentor and a role model for a long, long time. This would not be my first or last disappointment with politicians who make promises in order to get elected while stealing, cheating, and manipulating the system once in office. Sociopaths. What a shame!

THE BOOKIES

Revere was known as a breeding ground for organized crime and a large network of bookies. There was literally a bookie who would handle your action on almost every street corner, especially in the Italian sections of the city. Revere Street was no exception. I had become friends with a number of bookies in the area of the Soccorso Club.

One of my favorites was a guy named Loui. He owned a restaurant a few blocks from the club. I would usually go there on Saturdays to meet the mayor and some of his friends before heading to the football games. Loui's had some of the best Italian food I've ever had in my life!

I would also drop by Loui's new lounge that he opened up over the restaurant for happy hour or some late nighttime entertainment. He was both a bookie and an entrepreneur.

LEE'S TRAILER PARK

One day, Loui asked me to do a favor for him. I said yes with no hesitation as he was a friend and a good guy to be on the right side of. Loui peeled off five hundred dollars from his roll and handed it to me along with a slip of paper. The paper had a list of the bets I was to make on his behalf at the Wonderland Dog Track, which was only a few miles away from his restaurant and lounge. Apparently, Loui had received some inside information on the night's races (and the results thereof).

Everything I played for him was based on a sequenced contingency of betting. As an example, I was told to bet on the number-three dog in the first race and then to "wheel" that dog for the daily double. That meant that I was to bet the number-three dog in the first race with every dog in the second race, thereby assuring a daily double win—assuming, of course, that the number-three dog won the first race. I would also be paid off for the number-three dog winning the first race on his own.

If the daily double paid off, then I had a list of dogs to bet on in subsequent races. If it did not pay off, then I was to bet only the next two races as instructed and then return to Loui's place, win or lose.

It so happened that the number-three dog won the first race, assuring a daily double win as well. It would just be a matter of which dog won the second race and what the impact would be on the odds for the daily double payout.

I stuck around and made the other bets in the remaining races as instructed, some losing but most winning. I ended up with more than twenty-five hundred dollars in my pockets. Then it was back to Loui to give him his winnings. Naturally, I stopped at a club or two along the way to play the role of the big spaccone with the roll of cash in my hand. As odd as it may seem (and as stupid as it may seem), I never made the same bets that were on Loui's list. I just didn't feel that anything could be that solid. I bet my own dogs and ended up losing money for the evening.

I finally made it back to Loui's place and handed him his winnings. He wasn't thrilled that it took me so long to return. He said he heard through the grapevine that I was carousing around Revere Street instead of coming straight to him with the cash. No worries. Mission accomplished . . . or so I thought.

The next thing that happened made me wish I had worn some Depends that night. Loui sat down with his calculator and added everything up. "OK," he said. "There should be three grand here but there's only twenty-five hundred. What the hell did you do with the other five hundred?"

I went over it again and again and told him that I had made every bet, just as he instructed. "I didn't take any money and I didn't spend any of the winnings," I said.

Loui was getting hot—not a good position to be in with a bookie. Finally, a guy by the name of Tony Mer, who was watching what was going on, quietly walked over and said to Loui, "You forgot to take out the five hundred that he started with." Loui had just calculated the total winning lines and neglected to take into consideration the five hundred dollars I'd needed to start the bet ball rolling. In other words, there were some losing bets along the way . . . to the tune of five hundred dollars. I breathed a sigh of relief when Loui said, "Oh yeah, that's right." WHEW!

Loui said, "How'd you do, kid? You must have picked up some winnings as well.

Sheepishly, I told him, "No, actually I bet different dogs than were on the list."

"Don't give me that crap," Loui said. "I know you did pretty good. You're not that dumb." (Yeah, right.)

Anyway, no tip for being the bet messenger . . . just a shot of Galliano. Yuk! "When you lose, don't lose the lesson." Lesson learned: Don't try to outsmart those who are in the know, especially when you are dealing with their area of expertise. "The mind works like a parachute. It's at its best when it's open!"

MY BLOOD-BROTHER JOINS THE NAVY

It was 1966, and things were hot and heavy in Viet Nam. My blood-brother Bobby was concerned that he might get drafted and sent to the rice paddies as an infantryman. He became proactive and was thinking about enlisting, thereby giving himself some say as to where he might go and what he might be assigned to do in the service. There were three or four of us who were thinking along the same lines as Bobby. His parents added to the momentum by bringing a Navy recruiter to their trailer one night to meet with Bobby. It was "Anchors Aweigh" after that meeting, as Bobby joined the Navy.

It was a great decision for him. They assigned him to the Naval base in Corpus Christi, Texas, where he worked as an aircraft mechanic (a definite upgrade from the rice paddies). Not only did he not have to fight in the war, but he also met his future wife, Judy, in Texas.

I chose a different route and waited out the draft process. After all, it was a lottery, and there was a chance I might not be called up at all. There was also the fact that I was attending Northeastern and had a possible medical issue as well (asthma). I rolled the draft dice to see how it would work out for me. Eventually, I was called up but (thank God) not taken. Lucky outcome on my part.

With Bobby gone and me entering my twenties, it was time to leave Lee's Trailer Park and begin the next chapter of my life. And so I did.

J. H. JAMES

EPILOGUE

DAVE DYER

After leaving Maine and reestablishing Lee's Trailer Park as our new home, I would occasionally return to Scarborough, Maine, to spend the weekend with my good friend Dave Dyer. Our infamous road trips were still alive and well. Break out the cooler, Dave, I'm headed your way!

While the old adage, "Absence makes the heart grows fonder" is generally true, sometimes it is also true that "Familiarity breeds contempt." While Dave and I remained good friends, our 24/7 time together at Rouse's Point in upstate New York took somewhat of a toll on that friendship. While we enjoyed our occasional weekend road trips, things were never quite the same as they were prior to our time together in Rouse's Point.

Eventually, we drifted away from each other and went our separate ways. It was many years later when I tried to contact my old friend Dave to catch up on the twists and turns our lives had taken.

I was planning a business trip to South Portland, Maine, and wanted to spend some time with him while I was there. It was then that I learned he had unexpectedly passed away on February 1, 1988. He was only forty-one years old.

I only wish that I had attempted to see him again before he passed. As the lyrics in the old song "Time in a Bottle" by Steelers Wheel indicate, none of us can put time in a bottle to be used later on in life.

Lesson learned: Never hesitate to reach out to someone you care about when you find yourself thinking about them. When you finally try to connect, it could be too late. Once they are gone, you can't un-ring that bell.

BOBBY KELLY

Bobby Kelly married his wife, Judy, in 1968. They have three sons and live in Hudson, New Hampshire. He still has a boat and spends time on Lake Winnipesaukee during the New England summers. He also has a vacation home in Fort Meyers, Florida.

Unlike my friend Dave Dyer, Bobby and I have stayed in touch with each other for more than fifty years since going our separate ways. Our friendship dates back to when we were five years old, making it more than sixty-five years that we have known each other.

Last year, my wife, Ashlee, and I made a trip to Boston where we visited with Bobby and Judy and talked about the good old days. We drove through Lee's Trailer Park and visited some of our old stomping grounds in Revere. We also stopped by the gravesites of Mom and Tony, where we paid our respects to each of them.

There was a lunch at Bianchi's Pizza and Kelly's Roast Beef (no relation to Bobby). Then it was on to dinner at a great Italian restaurant in the North End, resulting in a renewed commitment to stay in touch and continue to visit each other for the duration. Bobby is threatening to visit us in Hawaii sometime soon. I hope he follows through, as it would be great to spend some time with them again. Note/reminder to self: You can't put time in a bottle.

LEE'S TRAILER PARK

TONY PACIULLI

My mom also eventually left Lee's Trailer Park. She bought a huge brick house at the top of a hill on Park Avenue in Revere. She had two tenants in separate apartments within the house and, yes, Tony was still a part of her life.

I was now out on my own and no longer living with Mom and Tony, although I still visited them on a fairly regular basis. Tony's health had faded dramatically. He could not get up and around like he had in years past. Apparently, his heart and his lifestyle were catching up with him. He spent most of his days in their bedroom until he could garner enough strength to make it to his car and head out on "business." Actually, he was determined not to stay in the house every day if he could avoid it.

Whether it was his failing health, neurosis, or a combination of the two, Tony was genuinely afraid of my mom. He was certain that she was going to do something bad to him, and he, therefore, lived in constant fear of her.

When I visited with them, I would sit on the edge of Tony's bed while he confided in me regarding his fear of Mom. While I tried to reassure him that she would not do anything to hurt him, I did not make much progress in that regard.

I think Tony eventually realized that he was nearing the end of his life. To the extent he could, he tried to make amends with me for some of the unhealed wounds of the past. He was never really a father figure for me and wasn't even legally my stepfather. That having been said, "it was what it was," and I tried to make the best of it. Lesson learned: We don't always get what we want in life. Sometimes we must do what we have to do rather than what we want to do. The "HAVE TO DOS" will eventually get us to our "WANT TO DOS."

Near the end, I had finally found a form of closure with Tony. We didn't become best of friends, however, I forgave him for what he did (and didn't do) to me and my mom throughout the years that he was a part of our lives.

Tony died in 1993. He was sixty-seven years old. I was a pallbearer at his funeral, along with three of his biological sons. I wore sunglasses and cried. I didn't want anyone to see or feel the pain that welled up within me for reasons that will always be beyond my understanding.

MOM

After Tony passed in 1993, Mom began to deteriorate emotionally and physically. She was consuming approximately a quart or more of Canadian Club whisky and smoking two packs of cigarettes per day. She was barely functional and could not keep up with the huge brick house and her tenants on Park Avenue in Revere.

I was living in Florida at the time and was constantly in touch with her. It had finally come time to take the bull by the horns and to step up and help Mom out of the situation she had put herself in.

I traveled to Boston and stayed with her while we put her house up for sale. Her job was to pace the floor and rub her hands together in a state of constant worry, anxiety, and negativity. She handled her job perfectly!

The plan was to sell the house and then move her to Florida where she could buy a condo so that I could keep a closer eye on her. No, she did not want to live with me and vice-versa. Besides, I had become a professional motivational speaker and was traveling throughout the country and the world. I needed to find her a place where she would be safe when something went wrong, which it inevitably would.

And then, the very best thing that's ever happened to me in my entire life occurred: My wife, Ashlee, became a part of it. She took very good care of Mom and was the only woman that I had ever been with whom Mom really loved.

Despite our best efforts, Mom's drinking, smoking, and early stages of dementia were winning the battle for her life. We placed Mom in an adult congregate living facility approximately a mile or two from where we lived. They had the medical facilities and therapists that could help her during these trying times. We could also visit with her two to three times a week and take her out for her favorite greasy hamburger on Saturdays.

Mom continued to deteriorate. She'd had a stint inserted in her heart twenty years earlier. She had part of her colon removed because of cancer. She had a lobe in her left lung removed because of cancer. She had an embolism that almost took her life. She broke her arm in a fall and severely banged her head into a doorknob during another incident. She was experiencing severe, uncontrollable muscle spasms and had virtually lost all of what little dexterity remained in her body. We could no longer even get her into the car for our Saturday hamburger junkets.

They finally moved Mom from the ACLF into the permanent care section of the facility. This was the beginning of the end that we all knew was coming. Mom passed away in October 2004. She was seventy-six years old.

Mom was an avid Red Sox fan. We used to sit on the stoop of her big brick house in Revere and look over toward Boston. We could see the lights from Fenway Park as we listened to the games on the radio.

Even when she was in her final stages, she would always ask me who was pitching on the days that I came to visit with her. Every once in a while, she would say, "He's a bum! Why do they even bother putting him on the mound!" She was a classic.

We cremated my mom after she passed. Ashlee and I took her ashes back to Boston where they were interned next to Tony's grave.

This was the year that the Red Sox finally won their first World Series in eighty-six years. Mom had died the week before the final game. I am confident that she had a front-row seat throughout the series. She didn't miss a pitch!

It is fair to say that Mom and I had a complicated relationship. I always felt as though I was somewhat of a burden to her. She was still a young woman, only twenty-four years old, when I was thrust upon her because of her leaving my dad.

Divorce was not a very fashionable or accepted way of life back in those days. There was definitely a stigma attached to being a female single parent.

While at the intellectual level I knew Mom loved me, she was never one for expressing her feelings in words or warm fuzzy hugs or deeds. That having been said, she came back for me at that farmhouse so many years ago and took me with her as she had promised. She nurtured me, fed me, clothed me, and took care of me for my entire young life. I will never forget her and will always love her.

ME

Even if I could, I would not change one day, one challenge, or one event in all the years that I lived in Lee's Trailer Park and in our home on wheels in Maine. As I mentioned earlier in this book, "That which doesn't kill you serves to strengthen you." The adversities I faced growing up without a father and living in poverty during my early childhood years helped to make me who I am today.

I now live in Hawaii with my wonderful wife, Ashlee, who has made me the happiest (and luckiest) man in the world. None of what I have today would have been possible without growing up in Lee's Trailer Park.

Yes, there have been many years and many challenges that followed the first chapter of my life in Lee's Trailer Park. Maybe I will share some of them with you in another book someday. For now, I know that I am blessed and that God truly loves me, despite some of the mistakes that I have made while traveling this road of life that we are all on. For me, it has been the philosophy of "keeping the faith" that has helped me to navigate the great rollercoaster of life. My greatest wish for all of you reading this book is that you will realize even one-half of the success, joy, and happiness I have experienced in my life. If you do, you will be thankful for, and blessed by, all of the great things that God sends your way.

Jesse "J. H." James

CPSIA information can be obtained
at www.ICGtesting.com
Printed in the USA
BVHW061934200822
645087BV00001B/127